# MANAGEMENT ACCOUNTING FOR THE LENDING BANKER

by

## M.A. PITCHER
FIB, ACIS, AMBIM

D1430748

THE INSTITUTE OF BANKERS
10 Lombard Street, London EC3V 9AS

First published in 1979 by
THE INSTITUTE OF BANKERS
10 Lombard Street, London EC3V 9AS

Reprinted 1980, 1983.

ISBN: 0 85297 050 1 (hardback)
ISBN: 0 85297 047 1 (paperback)

Printed and bound in England by
Stephen Austin & Sons Ltd/Hertford.

# Contents

# Acknowledgements

Six years ago I knew nothing about management accounting. That I now possess a little knowledge of the subject is due to many people unfortunately far too numerous to mention here individually. Nonetheless I am in their debt.

The following provided much valued comments when the book was in draft form and I gratefully acknowledge their kind help: M.J. Clipsham (Midland Bank); W.F.C. Hartley (Management Centre, University of Bradford); C. McEvoy and M.J. Robbie (Department of Management Studies, University of Technology, Loughborough); G.J. Payne; J.D. Smart (Lloyds Bank); and J. Tugwell (National Westminster Bank).

Whatever faults and inaccuracies remain are, of course, my own.

M.A.P.

# Preface

I make no grand claims for this book. It has been written by a very ordinary branch banker who was fortunate enough to be at the receiving end of a special training programme centred around the financial needs of the smaller business.

The book stems from a series of articles which appeared from the beginning of 1976 to mid-1978 in the *Journal of The Institute of Bankers*. The ground now covered is largely unchanged, although the absence of tight space considerations has allowed me to expand certain sections and to amend other areas where my original treatment demanded improvement. I hope that the appendices will also prove useful to readers.

No attempt has been made to produce a definitive work on management-accounting since a vast array of literature is readily available on this subject.

Instead, I have endeavoured to cover and illustrate the basic ideas in so far as they impinge upon the work of lending bankers, and readers are referred to other publications – some of which are listed among the references which follow most chapters – if they wish to become fully conversant with any particular topic. The books and articles mentioned are my own selection; they represent those that I have found most helpful.

I have attempted to stick closely to my subject and to avoid side issues, however important they might be. For example, little mention is made of inflation – or the tremendous amount of paper issuing forth on this subject from the accountancy profession – since the need for good management information has not just sprung out of the unusual conditions of the past few years. Management accounting is always desirable as an aid to business success; in times like the present it becomes essential.

I have tried to keep it simple: partly out of necessity and partly because of a comment made to me several years ago by a member of the Institute of Cost and Management Accountants that 'eighty per cent of management accounting is commonsense'.

When asked 'and what market are you aiming at' I can only reply that the book is intended for people at any stage of their banking career who, like myself, would like to know more about lending money successfully. I hope, for my publisher's sake, that I am not in a minority of one! Although this could never be a straightforward textbook for the student, I have tried to pay some heed to the Institute of Bankers' new syllabuses, particularly the Practice of Banking 3 and the Business Planning and Control sections in the Financial Studies Diploma.

Three final points. First, to avoid tiresome repetition, I have chosen to ignore my training and have used the terms 'company', 'business' and 'firm' fairly indiscriminately to mean any commercial or industrial enterprise. Secondly, by attempting to link traditional methods of credit analysis with newer financial techniques, I have placed what are virtually unassailable basic concepts from the area of management accounting alongside ideas on certain aspects of bank lending that represent my personal opinions and are, therefore, by no means sacrosanct. I hope that this intermingling of basic concepts with some of my own views will not destroy any value the book might otherwise have for those who hold contrary views. My own views will normally be indicated by a specific reference or by using the first person singular. Thirdly, the experience on which this book is based stems directly from my close association with Barclays Business Advisory Service over the years 1972-5, and most of my general comments relate to businesses in the small to medium-sized range – in broad terms, those with an annual turnover of £5 million or less. Few of the concepts change when applied to the larger firm, although they usually become more sophisticated in design and more complicated to administer. The cases referred to in this book are drawn from my own experience, but all names, locations and occupations have been altered to preserve anonymity.

*Michael Pitcher*
*Crowthorne*
*June 1978*

# CHAPTER 1

# Introduction

## 1.1. LENDING MONEY SUCCESSFULLY – A PRIME SKILL

If the prime skill of a banker is concerned with the successful lending of money – and I suspect that few people reading these words would wish to deny that this is the case – then this book is directed at the heart of banking. It seeks to build on the sound foundations of traditional methods of credit assessment by using the newer bricks of management accounting.

I say sound foundations because there is nothing within these covers that sets out to destroy the old. Indeed, the opposite is true. An attempt is made to show that newer techniques, when used in conjunction with established methods of analysis, can improve lending decisions by providing a much fuller picture of all the circumstances surrounding an existing or potential borrowing and provide a surer means of control during the life of the facility. This view does not make older views obsolete; it strengthens and reinforces them. The theme is not that traditional methods are inappropriate, but that they may be insufficient in certain circumstances.

Most books on the subject open by describing what management accounting is, emphasising those aspects which distinguish it from financial accounting. I intend leaving such a description until Chapter 3, since I feel that unless the traditional tools of credit analysis can be found wanting in some way then there is no incentive to examine different techniques. Change for its own sake is a doctrine which attracts few disciples. Any acceptance of the assistance that may be offered by the areas to be discussed depends on an agreement that the present information base for many lendings is inadequate or that we may be missing good opportunities for increasing our advances total by adopting an approach that concentrates on only a few of the overall strengths and weaknesses of a business enterprise.

The remainder of this chapter examines these thoughts in more detail.

## 1.2.  THE CHANGING ROLE OF THE LENDING BANKER

We are continually being told that we live in a rapidly changing world, with that well-known old Chinese proverb about the only constant thing in life being brought out ad nauseam. Although the pace of such change is often overstated, few would deny that the day-to-day life of a lending banker (particularly those based in branches) has altered appreciably over the past decade. The previously smouldering embers of competition have been fanned by winds from many directions. An important spur to the clearing banks has come from the pressure of other banks, particularly those from North America with their different concepts of lending styles and marketing opportunities. The growth of a wide range of ancilliary in-house lending services has increased the complexity of the daily round. The quiet revolution of term lending has brought forth a need for skills of a different kind. And, most importantly, on top of all this has been the growing sophistication of our corporate customers: this has been a patchwork affair with the brighter colours of improved financial planning and control much more clearly visible in certain sectors than in others, but the fact that a pattern of progress has emerged is undeniable.

The branch banker's role then is surely changing from the mere merchant in money described by writers of the past. Gilbart's description of 'a dealer in capital . . . an intermediate party between the borrower and the lender'[1] looks somewhat inadequate compared with the much broader responsibilities the modern banker is expected to shoulder. He is actively encouraged to leave the sanctuary of his office in order to seek out and attempt to solve the problems of his customers, both actual and potential. And he has increasingly needed to become involved with the profitable growth of his customers.

No doubt the arguments over the extent to which this co-operation should progress will continue over the years to provide the fuel for much heated debate. How far should a banker go in directing the operations of a business customer or making suggestions about their future path? How much should we assume the mantle of company management? I do not pretend to know the answers to these questions, but I do know that banks only survive and prosper if their customers do likewise. I can see few objections to viewing the customer/banker relationship as a kind of mutually beneficial partnership with both parties having something to gain from each other's strengths. To refuse to accept that we have any *direct* interest in the future success of our business customers – and in any temporary setbacks they may encounter on the way – cannot surely be in the best interest of any bank in today's conditions. And is enlightened self-interest a policy to be ashamed of at any time?

To my mind, the major question posed by this changing scene is: has our range of lending services and spread of related skills altered to meet the new needs in the market place? Although it can be said with some justification that we have clung to the traditional over-draft for too long and expected too much from it, many exciting and far-reaching innovations have come out of the financial services sector over the past decade and it would be hard to fault on this score an industry where evolution rather than revolution will long be the order of the day. So far as any improvement in our range of skills is concerned, I believe that the banks' performance has been less praiseworthy. There have been few, if any, changes to the yardsticks used by clearing bankers in judging a lending proposition, and the often heard remark that 'banks lend money as they did 100 years ago' must carry some validity. Has the training of lending bankers kept pace with the changing environment? Many would say not. In 1975 the senior general manager of a large clearing bank commented that 'The corporate finance training of many clearing bankers is narrow, a little old-fashioned and historically orientated in terms of the information base of company accounts. It should be based on more depth and on a projection and management accounts base'.[2] Is what has really happened that banks have attempted to meet the new conditions by dressing their managers in a new suit of clothes, but failing to change the inner man? Above all, is our lending policy too restrictive and negative in approach, bearing in mind that in normal times one of any bank's major objectives must be to increase its lending subject to the usual criteria of safety, profitability and liquidity?

## 1.3. THE CUSTOMER'S POINT OF VIEW

I have often wondered whether we spend sufficient time and effort in discovering how we appear to our customers. All too frequently I have gained the impression from books, articles and in general discussion that banks are doing their customers a favour in lending them money and that it is an impertinence to suggest that the reverse might be true.

How do our attitudes to lending look from the customers' angle? Do they see us as prime suppliers of one of the most crucial raw materials required by their business; always approachable; ever sympathetic; understanding their problems almost as soon as they arise; prepared to take the extra risk where the situation warrants it? Or do they see the opposite image? Do they liken us to a bunch of Shylocks; never stepping outside of the rulebook; always adopting a 'belt and braces' approach; paused ever ready to snatch the umbrella away as soon as clouds begin to gather on the horizon?

The answer, as always, must lie between these two extremes, but is it closer to the latter than we would wish? It is partly a communications problem since we rarely go out of our way to explain how we view matters from our side of the fence; I have often been surprised at how little even qualified commercial people such as accountants know about the guidelines used by a banker when assessing a lending proposal. But is it also partly due to the fact that we have been looking almost exclusively for a certain type of security: asset backing that can be sold for sufficient to repay our debt in case of need? How should we react to the charge that 'clearing banks come closest to a pure liquidation approach . . . there seems to be no systematic gathering of information and forecasts'[3] or 'the overdraft system may . . . have prompted an unnecessarily conservative lending approach'?[4]

I see nothing against pawnbroking. The property crisis of the past few years has shown that this type of lending may not always be as risk-free as many had imagined, but if it is profitable and meets a need then long may it have a place in a banker's range of services. But is there nothing else? Are there no other opportunities for safe lending? Is there a danger in justifying a loan purely because of the value of the asset backing? Remembering that risk is closely related to uncertainty, can we not obtain another kind of security – perhaps complementary to the first – which comes from knowing what is happening inside a business, on a regular basis, and being kept informed of management's plans for the future? How much more satisfying to see our money being used successfully in a going concern; how much more reassuring to know that our investment is generating the cash flow required for repayment; and how much better for the long-term prospects of a bank in building a spirit of mutual trust based on closer co-operation.

Certain types of traditional security may now need rethinking. As an example, the formal debenture is a potent weapon in a banker's armoury providing as it does such an all-embracing defence against the outside world, apart from those pertinacious preferential creditors who take precedence over any floating assets charged. Is such blanket coverage fair to our customers, who are effectively debarred from raising money elsewhere except at our pleasure, or to other outside creditors all but a few of whom will be customers of a UK bank?

## 1.4. THE PLACE OF MANAGEMENT ACCOUNTING

Let me start by saying what management accounting is not. It is not a panacea for all ills. No such strong medicine exists. It cannot guarantee success or provide a miracle cure. Neither can it answer all the lending banker's questions. It has its limitations and short-comings just as do the more traditional aids to credit analysis.

It is only as accurate and useful as the people producing and using it choose to make it. The best information can do little to help managers intent on ignoring it and continuing to make decisions wherever fancy leads them. It also relies on the continuing commitment of management, as major benefits are usually seen only in the medium and long term.

Where then does the value of management accounting information fit into the changing pattern described earlier? Management accounting can open up the dark, hidden areas in a company. It can highlight certain strengths and weaknesses almost as soon as they occur. It can then provide the means for a proper system of financial planning and control which in turn can supply the basis for informed decisions and improved monitoring ability.

Although it is difficult to conceive of any lending situation where well-compiled internally produced information would not be of interest to a banker, I am certainly not suggesting that it should be demanded in every case. The large, successful public company, for example, may well object to providing detailed forecasts which are not available to other outside parties (whether such secrecy is in the best interests of their shareholders is of course another matter) particularly if they simply require reasonable overdraft facilities for normal trading needs. In the current lending environment they could expect to be able to obtain this money elsewhere without providing such information and a request of this nature would merely cause annoyance. I almost suspect that in certain circles a trend is developing where such items as cash flow forecasts are *insisted* upon as support for virtually any advance. To my mind, this is completely wrong: we should *demand* suitable information when it is required for a lending decision and/or subsequent monitoring, but only *encourage* its production at other times. The trend must be allowed to evolve over a number of years if we are not to run the risk of unnecessarily upsetting our customers.

At present I see management accounting information being of special value to bankers in the following types of situation:

**a. New lendings** – either those requested by existing customers or on offer from potential customers proposing to transfer from other banks. Those from the latter source produce a higher-than-average crop of fresh bad debts for the recipient bank and thus usually demand a closer examination utilising all the information which can be extracted from the company.

**b. The rapidly growing company** – financial needs may well be outstripping the available asset cover normally required by bankers. There is danger in this situation of course: some will fail while others succeed. The skill comes in picking the right ones to back.

**c. Monitoring the progress of all but the safest advances** – here it is difficult to provide a specific definition of the accounts I have in mind. It covers all those advances where adequate control cannot be maintained by relying solely on the audited figures and the run of the banking account. Most modern commentators agree that, contrary to the opinion promulgated by the mass media, businesses go bust *slowly*. They rarely expire suddenly one wet Wednesday afternoon without the warning signs having been there for many months, or even years, for those who were prepared to seek them.

**d. Where the management appears ill-informed** – many bankers say that the business acumen of the directors is of the greatest importance. I would agree entirely with this view, questioning only whether our assessment of their expertise is not frequently a subjective one. Without first judging the quality of the information on which they base their decisions it is difficult for the assessment to be otherwise.

**e. Business development** – in its broadest sense the profitable growth of his branch must be the ultimate objective of every bank official. Some of the areas covered in this book should provide the means to develop a closer understanding between ourselves and both existing and potential customers. This can surely do nothing but aid a banker's attempts to gain new business.

These, then, are some examples. They are not in self-contained compartments and many accounts will fall into more than one category.

# References

[1] *Elements of Banking: a selection from J.W. Gilbart's 'A Practical Treatise on Banking'*. Edited by S.J.H. van Hengel. Kruseman: The Hague, 1967.
[2] Weyer, D.V.: 'The Changing Role of the Clearing Banks in Society'. *Journal of The Institute of Bankers*, April 1975.
[3] Donaldson, T.H.: 'Banking for a Going Concern – principles of sound lending'. *Journal of The Institute of Bankers*, February 1977.
[4] 'The limited usefulness of security'. *The Economist*, 9 October 1976.

CHAPTER 2

# Shortcomings of Traditional Methods of Credit Analysis

## 2.1. BASIC PRINCIPLES OF LENDING

It has already been said that management accounting can never replace the existing methods of credit assessment which have served bankers so well over the years. The aim of this chapter is to examine whether these established lending aids have important shortcomings – some surprisingly under-publicised – which in certain situations render them in need of support.

How do bankers arrive at a lending decision? What are the predominant questions and criteria passing through their minds when they are confronted with a request for an advance? For those of us not possessing some mystical second-sight, it is probably a combination of the three C's – character, capability and capital – and four basic questions along the following lines:
– How much is required?
– What is to be done with the money?
– What are the plans for repayment?
– What will be the bank's position if the plans for repayment go wrong?

Of course there will be many subsidiary questions to ask before these main ones can be answered, but my point at this stage is: how important are these considerations and how well developed is our ability, or that of our customers, to provide the answers needed?

The *character* of the borrower will always be a prime factor in any lending decision but, in my view, its importance is frequently over-stressed. Time and again during my banking career I have heard colleagues assert that they 'lend to the man' and that considerations of honesty and integrity far outweigh any judgement they may make on an analysis of any financial information which may be available.

Honesty, unfortunately, is simply not enough to ensure the success of an enterprise as many businessmen are discovering to their distress in the difficult and demanding conditions of today. All the integrity in the world will be of little help to the managers of a company that is rapidly sinking into oblivion because they have not adapted their product range to meet the needs of a changing market or taken corrective action to counter a disproportionate rise in overhead costs.

I do not want to be misunderstood on this point. I am not suggesting that we should lend to rogues, but rather that honesty does not always equate with creditworthiness.

*Capability* is another key area of concern and it provides the opportunity to introduce an idea which is of great relevance to bankers. Most businesses are capable in a manufacturing sense; they tend to be good at producing things. They take a justifiable pride in the product of their labours and enjoy the whole of the manufacturing process. But often they are much less capable in a financial sense; they tend to have little understanding of the underlying financial state of their business until outside pressures are placed upon them, e.g. a forceful demand from creditors or a threatening letter from their bank manager notifying them of an excess position. It is a fundamental mistake to assume that a businessman knows his business, particularly at the small and medium-sized end of the market. Many, for example, have little or no real idea of where their break-even point is likely to occur, or the current state of their profitability. Most lack the knowledge or the inclination to produce the relevant figures. A large number of businesses seek to excuse the absence of such information by suggesting that they have a 'feel' for the way the business is going. Yet time and again I have seen examples of companies honestly believing they were earning profits, only to find them quickly converted into losses when up-to-date figures were extracted to reveal the true position. Many then stated quite categorically that good profits would be seen during the coming six months, only for budgets to be produced showing a potential loss for the period.

*Capital* is always required for any business. Bankers will always be concerned to ensure that their investment bears a reasonable relationship to the amount of the proprietor's stake. Apart from any other consideration, the risk of losing one's own capital is a powerful incentive to get things right. But do existing methods of assessment provide sufficient help in deciding how much, for how long, and of what type?

Turning next to the four basic banking questions, my contention is that, because of the limited ability on the part of both bank and customer to answer the first three of these, we tend to concentrate on the last aspect – security. Most of us learn during our training that this is one of the less important aspects of a lending proposition, but to many of our customers it often appears to be an overriding factor in the forefront of our minds when we view their request and a prerequisite for any meaningful discussion. I can well remember an old manager telling me soon after I joined the bank, 'Don't let security influence a lending decision; I never lend money with security that I wouldn't lend without'. An oversimplification perhaps, but a message I cling to nonetheless as one that I have heard only infrequently during my career.

In spite of their early protestations to the contrary, the authors of most banking textbooks are very concerned with security, be it the calculation of the surplus in a balance sheet coupled with advice on when to take a debenture, or the nature of the charge required over a sublease held in the names of trustees. Such emphasis on security is surely undesirable? It inhibits our attempts to develop more sophisticated methods of examining how our money is being used in a business and how and when repayment will be achieved. Lending against tangible security has its place, but to concentrate on it exclusively must restrict unfairly the flow of bank finance to soundly-controlled enterprises which could borrow funds successfully if only they possessed the necessary asset backing to pledge as collateral.

## 2.2. THE AUDITED ACCOUNTS

The audited figures must certainly rank as the most used lending tool of all. Many eminent bankers have produced excellent works on their use and value and they are, quite rightly, highly regarded as a means of understanding the state of affairs of a company quickly and easily. They can answer many of the questions that surround a lending proposition and it would be foolhardy to suggest that the information they contain can be ignored by any banker.

But are they not often overworked in an attempt to extract more value than is theirs to give? To say that they suffer from important limitations is to suggest nothing new to the lending banker, but I wonder how often we pause to consider the severity of their shortcomings. The following list is a brief summary only and it is compiled in no particular order of importance. Many of the areas discussed are interrelated:

**a. The figures look backwards, not forwards.** Obviously the past performance of customers should not be disregarded, but it is useful only when it helps forecast their likely future achievements. Using historical data as the sole basis of judgement on a lending proposal has been likened to attempting to drive a car looking only at the rearview-mirror.

**b. They are out of date by the time they are seen by bank and customer.** Some delay is inevitable because an audit cannot be completed within minutes of the end of the financial year of a business. The average time-lag at the moment appears to be in the region of six to nine months,[1] with delays of eighteen months or more not uncommon. The position is, however, often more serious than it appears at first sight. A company whose year end is, say, 31 December 1977, may show a reasonable profit when the accounts become available during December 1978. But this profit may all have been earned during the first half of 1977 since which time the business has been incurring an undetected loss. The loss-making could continue on an ever-increasing scale without anyone's knowledge until the 1978 accounts are available in December 1979 – some 30 months after the time when the company first stopped earning profits. The position may be discovered earlier if a liquidity crisis occurs, but by then it is often too late.

**c. They only show assets and liabilities that can be measured in financial terms.** No mention may be made, for example, of:
– The quality of the management, the age and health of the directors, what succession is being cultivated? managerial style.
– Aspects of the labour force, is recruitment of the right type of skilled/unskilled employee easy or difficult? how are relations with the unions?
– The presence of assets which have been fully depreciated but which may still possess some value, the condition of the plant and machinery, the extent to which capacity is underutilised.
– The company's trading environment, what legislative, economic or social constraints affect the business? is it well or poorly located?
– What is happening to the markets? is the product range altering to meet the changing needs of the consumer?
Readers will, no doubt, be able to think of many more examples.

**d. At present, the normal financial measure used is one which relates assets to their original cost and not their resale value or replacement cost.** The two main exceptions to this principle are:
– If it is thought that current assets will fetch less than their cost

price, then they are shown at their net realisable value.

– When items are purchased for continuing use in the business and not for resale (fixed assets), then they are stated at cost less any depreciation which may be considered necessary.

While being commendable in some ways, this attitude of conservatism (or is it optimism?) in accounting practice can lead to gross misstatements in the financial standing of an enterprise.[2]

**e. The accounts are often produced for tax purposes.** It is impossible to make precise comments under this heading since little empirical research has been carried out in the area. Some authorities suggest that the practice is not widespread and where it does exist the customer deserves a cold shoulder from his banker. I can only say that in my experience few smaller companies do not 'massage' their reported figures in order to pay as little tax as possible, and my branch would have been a very uncrowded place if I had shown all of them the door.

There are a number of possibilities for such manipulation; two of the most frequently encountered are:

– Stock – in many cases this is shown in the accounts at directors' valuation and the figure is accepted by the auditor without verification. The implications are obvious, although following the introduction of tax deferrals on stock increases conservatism cannot be assumed.

– Sales – achieved quite simply by carrying forward sales invoices into the next accounting period thereby reducing profit.

It must be emphasised that these practices are not necessarily fraudulent or even intentional. I once visited one business holding large quantities of raw materials, work-in-progress and finished goods, where the stock had not been counted for seven years! The managers simply had no idea of the true value and their audited accounts (and any internal management accounts had they been produced) could only be extracted by using very broad estimates. Consider also the sometimes enormous differences which can occur in a balance sheet and the reported after-tax profit if an auditor chooses to use a deferred tax account.[3]

All too frequently neither customer nor banker calculate the longer-term effect of many of these tax avoidance procedures. This restricts the value of the accounts to outsiders and provides little help to the managers in the running of their business.

**f. The accounts are a snapshot of a business at a moment in time.** Take a picture the following day and the scene may look very different. As with many of us, companies like to look their best when they are photographed and sometimes dress for the occasion. 'Ratio-juggling' is a common example of what I have in mind – a practice not unknown to banks – but 'creative' or 'cosmetic' accounting has been known to take many forms. To name a few:

– Capitalising revenue expenditure. This has been called the 'oldest trick in the book'[4] and involves bringing into the balance sheet as an asset certain expenditure which might reasonably have been taken into the profit and loss account instead, thus improving profit for the year. One classic example is Rolls-Royce which, before the infamous collapse, kept its reported earnings up for several years by not treating research and development as an expense to be charged against trading profit.

– Cancelling out extraordinary losses by a transfer from reserves or making sure that an extraordinary credit appears in the same year, possibly by revaluing land and buildings.

– Changing the basis of stock valuation from one year to the next. The Inland Revenue's microscope will be brought in if this happens too frequently, but as a once-and-for-all exercise in a bad year it can work wonders.

g. Last, but by no means least, **most forms of accounting allow a considerable degree of interpretation to the individual or firm compiling the figures.** Auditors aim to produce figures which, in their opinion, reveal a true and fair view of the financial position of a business at a moment in time: and the word to stress is *view*. The work of auditors is not controlled by a massive weight of detailed legislation – quite the opposite. They have considerable leeway in which to exercise their judgement. There are numerous examples of different firms of auditors having vastly divergent views on the same set of books.

In this connection it is worth listing the examples mentioned in the Accounting Standards Committee's *Statement of Standard Accounting Practice No. 2* (SSAP 2)[5] of areas where different accounting bases are recognised which may have a significant effect on the reported results and general financial position of a business:

'Depreciation of fixed assets.
Treatment and amortisation of intangibles such as research and development expenditure, patents and trademarks.
Stocks and work-in-progress.
Long-term contracts.
Deferred taxation.

Hire purchase or instalment transactions.
Leasing and rental transactions.
Conversion of foreign currencies.
Repairs and renewals.
Consolidation policies.
Property development transactions.
Warranties for products or services.'

## 2.3. THE BANKING ACCOUNT

Traditionally the run of the current account has been viewed as a valuable lending tool and there is no doubt that clearing bankers are usually in the fortunate position of being able to tap a helpful source of information which is usually denied to other financial institutions.

But how useful is it? It can only provide information on past events and is often examined closely only when a review of the facility is due or a crisis point has been reached. In addition certain myths have grown up around its use that may be a hindrance to any banker concerned to see his money working in a successful business.

### Working capital needs

Thousands of applications must be submitted each year with 'working capital' as the purpose of the advance (or 'normal trading finance' as it is more correctly termed – the difference is purely semantic as it does not alter the way the money is actually spent within the business).

How then do we assess with any accuracy the working capital requirements of a business, having already said that one of the most important basic banking questions concerns the amount to be borrowed? Most of us have been trained to produce a figure from a balance sheet using a predetermined formula, but has this much value bearing in mind the deficiencies which exist in audited accounts, and does it not assume a much too static concept of the liquidity needs of a business? In the real world, surely, the composition of current assets and their relationship to current liabilities is constantly changing and with them the working capital requirement of a business.

Is it not the case that we lend most of our short-term money to customers to top up their requirements for cash and that we are usually unaware at the time of sanction how much will be used to increase current assets, reduce liabilities or purchase fixed assets? In practice, all three types of transaction take place on almost every business account simply because customers have a cheque **book** which they use for all purposes. It is a myth to assume that bank overdraft finance is normally used purely for expenditure 'above the line'. Frequently there is little point in turning to the customers for help as they often have little appreciation of a banker's position or their own real needs: they commonly ask for an increase in their facility because they see commitments arising a little way ahead which they cannot imagine they can cope with inside their existing limit.

A banker's main concern is the customer's ability to repay. This must be the prime quality that any lending can possess and it is the reason for generations of bankers seeking to insist that their money is only used for working capital purposes. My contention is that so long as this vital feature is present the traditional distinction between the finance of current and fixed assets is unimportant. To those bankers who may feel this is heresy I would say that it merely recognises what has happened in reality for many years. It does mean, however, that the ability to plan and control cash needs becomes of paramount importance and this will be examined in later chapters.

As a general point I believe that much more research is required in this area. The traditional banking ratios have been accepted for too long without thorough examination. Is it logical to accept that they can apply to all industries at all times?

## Solid and swinging accounts

As a corollary of the arguments on working capital needs, how able are we to assess the reasons for the development of a hard core position?

To suggest that a company having an overdraft limit of £100,000 within which the actual borrowing fluctuates between £20,000 and £95,000 during the term of sanction is using a portion of the bank's money incorrectly is, in my view, to adopt an altogether too simplistic view. Surely it is unreasonable to insist that longer-term finance be found for the £20,000 hard core if it is certain that the money is being used to finance stocks which are turning over at a reasonable rate. It must all depend on the circumstances of each individual case of course, but my point is that there may be no direct connection between the solid part of an overdraft and the amount a company has spent on purchasing non-current assets and repaying longer-term liabilities.

Once again, there appears to be a strong incentive for examining techniques which can assist both bankers and customers in forecasting and measuring the real financial needs of a business.

## 2.4. CONCLUSION

Management accounting cannot help with all the shortcomings mentioned in this chapter. But it can assist with some. And in any case there should be some benefit in examining the major inadequacies of the traditional tools of credit analysis on which so many of us rely.

In particular, I have stressed the limitations of audited accounts and, indeed, I shall come back to the subject in later chapters. There is not, and never will be, one immutable and inviolate profit figure for a business; there cannot be *the* profit, only *a* profit which may be subject to the judgements and tinkerings mentioned earlier.

This situation has long been recognised by auditors who are under few misconceptions as to the value of the figures they produce:

'In accountancy the term profit has no absolute meaning . . . The measurement is a subjective one in so far as it depends upon the view taken as to what the business has in fact set out to achieve. Thus the term "profit" as used by accountants can never have the absolute meaning which lawyers, economists and Revenue officials seek to attribute to it.'[6]

To that list may be added bankers.

### References and notes

[1] On the basis of a survey of 82 bank branches, D.A. Egginton, in his book *Accounting for the Banker,* Longman, 1977, suggests an average of seven months' delay from the end of the financial year until the accounts are in the hands of the banker.

[2] At the time of writing, the best way of overcoming the problems caused by the historic cost convention is the subject of lengthy debate.

[3] Another area which has been the subject of much disagreement both within and outside of the accountancy profession. The mechanics of a deferred tax account are well explained by D.A. Egginton, in *Accounting for the Banker, op. cit.* N.B. This disagreement has been partially resolved by the publication of *Statement of Standard Accounting Practice No. 15 (SSAP 15): Accounting for Deferred Taxation.* Published by the Institute of Chartered Accountants in England and Wales, October 1978.

[4] The practice was thus described by William Phillips in 'Company Accounts: when window dressing goes too far'. *Investors Chronicle,* 30 April 1976. This article contained 18 examples of 'creative' accounting.

[5] Accounting Standards Committee: *Statement of Standard Accounting Practice No. 2 (SSAP 2): Disclosure of Accounting Policies.* The Institute of Chartered Accountants in England and Wales, November 1971.

[6] Morison, A.M.C.: 'The Role of the Reporting Accountant Today'. *Accountancy,* January 1971.

CHAPTER 3

# What is Management Accounting?

## 3.1. THE INFORMATION GATHERER

Management accounting is not new. Some of the techniques have been used for many decades. Its formal introduction to this country came in 1950 from a British team of accountants following a tour of the United States. The concepts are well tested and they have become increasingly fashionable and accepted over the past 25 years.

There are numerous definitions of management accounting, every author appearing to feel duty-bound to provide his own. None are very helpful, but for the sake of completeness one is included which has the virtue of simplicity:

'the application of accounting techniques to the provision of information designed to assist all levels of management in *planning* and *controlling* the activities of the firm'.[1]

Certain aspects of this definition merit further examination. First and foremost, management accounting is concerned with the needs of management. Quite what management is and what managers are expected to do are questions for which there are probably as many answers as there are people questioned. But it has a lot to do with making decisions about scarce resources in uncertain situations. It is concerned with the future rather than the past. To practice his art a manager requires information of the right type, in the right quantity, at the right time. He cannot allocate resources effectively in a vacuum. Management accounting helps him by making available just sufficient information for the decision he is required to take. It provides the questions rather than the answers and has as its prime function the gathering of information. A management accountant in industry can rightly be referred to as an *information manager*.

The words 'planning' and 'control' require brief explanation as they will be used many times in later chapters. Once again definitions abound, but in broad terms planning is the selection of objectives and the means of achieving them; it involves choosing from alternatives. Control means checking actual results against planned results, with a view to ensuring satisfactory performance and possibly producing feedback which will assist with the review of plans. It should lead to taking action to correct any unsatisfactory area of performance.

In summary:

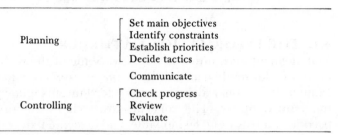

| Planning | Set main objectives |
| | Identify constraints |
| | Establish priorities |
| | Decide tactics |
| | |
| | Communicate |
| | |
| Controlling | Check progress |
| | Review |
| | Evaluate |

Many seasoned bankers may feel that all this has little relevance for their smaller business customers who are often paddling so furiously just to keep their heads above water that they have no time to spare for such theoretical and abstract ideas. I always think of the story of the wood-cutter whenever this objection is raised. A man was watching a wood-cutter working very hard on a hot summer's day. After several trees had been felled, the wood-cutter paused for a few minutes rest during which time the onlooker took the opportunity to say, 'I hope you won't mind my mentioning this, but you would get those trees down much faster if only you sharpened your axe'. 'I haven't got time for that,' replied the wood-cutter irritably, 'I've got 12 more trees to fell before I leave today and I'm already behind because this axe is so blunt.'

There are many decisions which businessmen find more difficult than they need because they never pause to consider that there might be a better and easier way. And certain problems might never arise if the correct course of action had been recommended at the outset. Good information is like a sharp axe: you use less effort in obtaining a better reward. How does a businessman make decisions about the future shape of his product mix unless he has up-to-date information on his present spread of sales? How does he make an investment in new machinery or plant without knowing how the purchase will affect his cost structure? And does he not require some forecast of how these and similar changes will alter demands on the financial resources of the business?

## 3.2. DISTINCTION BETWEEN FINANCIAL ACCOUNTING AND MANAGEMENT ACCOUNTING

Using these thoughts as a backcloth, a distinction can be drawn between financial accounting (i.e. the audited figures) and management accounting, although in the broadest sense any accounting information which is of value to the managers of an enterprise may be called management accounting.

### a. Financial accounting

The prime concern of financial accounting is to report historical information to interested parties who are outside of the business. The information produced is governed by generally accepted accounting principles, few of which are codified in any act of parliament. The overall intention is to comply with the provisions of the Companies Acts and present a true and fair view of the financial affairs of a company.

It cannot be emphasised too strongly that the loose rules which act as a framework for auditors only represent commonly agreed ways of presenting financial information and allow considerable room for differing interpretations.

The main forms in which this information is supplied are the balance sheet, the profit and loss account and the directors' report.

### b. Management accounting

Management accounting is at the opposite end of the information spectrum: the emphasis is totally different. It is primarily concerned with supplying people inside the company with up-to-date, relevant information on the immediate past and projections for the future. It acts as an important aid to decision making and enables the managers of a business to monitor and control its progress against a predetermined plan. Its prime aim is to assist managers in making their business more successful and it should only be produced if it is *useful*. Put simply: ' . . . in management accounting . . . the main test is not "Does the information conform to generally accepted accounting principles?" but "Is the information useful to the management of the company?" '[2]

The figures are produced for internal use; they need not and should not be doctored for external consumption. There is no incentive for the managers of a business to manipulate the facts; they only mislead themselves and make the task of steering the business needlessly difficult. This has enormous implications for the lending banker if he is on sufficiently good terms with his customer to request and be given such information.

The roles of the two types of accountant are very different and it is worth bearing in mind that financial accountants may find the transition difficult.

## c. Summarising the differences

**Financial accounting**

*i*   Historical.
Audited accounts covering the previous year's trading. Looks backwards not forwards.

*ii*   For outsiders.
Shareholders, loan and trade creditors, Inland Revenue, Registrar of Companies.

*iii*   Outsiders make the rules.
Professional bodies, e.g. Accounting Standards Committee, lay down the accounting principles. Must conform to disclosure requirements of the Companies Acts.

*iv*   Main report criterion –
True and Fair?
Financial reports should give a 'true and fair view' of a company's affairs.

*v*   Timing not critical.
Customary to prepare accounts once a year and little urgency over production in finished form.

**Management accounting**

*i*   Recent past and future.
Regular performance reports containing information on recent past and projections for future trends. Must be available soon after the event.

*ii*   For insiders.
Managers and directors.

*iii*   Insiders make the rules.
Content of reports and principles used can be suited to the company's activities and requirements of managers.

*iv*   Main report criterion –
Useful?
Does the information enable the management of the company to conduct its operations more effectively?

*v*   Timing of importance.
Accounts prepared as frequently as circumstances demand, and speed often vital.

## 3.3.   AN ACTUAL CASE

These thoughts on the shortcomings of established lending tools stem directly from my dealings with small and medium-sized businesses over the years. On innumerable occasions firms were heading for serious problems of which they were blissfully unaware; no warning bells were being set off by the audited figures or the run of the bank account.

This is such a case:

*XL Engineering Co. Ltd* is a light engineering business formed during the last war operating from a freehold factory in the Midlands. It has a history of steady and profitable growth. Occasional overdraft facilities have been readily agreed and equally promptly repaid in accordance with the arrangement.

The last three years' audited accounts reveal a healthy
position:

(All figures in '000s)

|  | June 1975 | June 1976 | June 1977 |
|---|---|---|---|
| **Current assets** | | | |
| Cash | 2.0 | 74.0 | 114.0 |
| Debtors | 150.0 | 164.0 | 202.0 |
| Stock | 125.0 | 134.0 | 212.0 |
|  | 277.0 | 372.0 | 528.0 |
| **Less current liabilities** | | | |
| Bank | 2.0 | | |
| Creditors | 45.0 | 74.0 | 151.0 |
| Directors' current accounts | 20.0 | 34.0 | 34.0 |
| Current taxation | 19.0 | 30.0 | 35.0 |
|  | 86.0 | 138.0 | 220.0 |
| Liquid surplus | 191.0 | 234.0 | 308.0 |
| **Fixed and other assets** | | | |
| Land & buildings | 100.0 | 100.0 | 100.0 |
| Plant & machinery | 6.0 | 6.0 | 6.0 |
| Fixtures & fittings | 2.5 | 2.1 | 2.1 |
| Motor vehicles | 15.0 | 18.0 | 14.0 |
|  | 123.5 | 126.1 | 122.1 |
| Total net assests | 314.5 | 360.1 | 430.1 |
| **Financed by:** | | | |
| **Term liabilities** | | | |
| Future taxation | 30.0 | 35.0 | 54.0 |
| **Capital** | | | |
| Ordinary | 0.4 | 0.4 | 0.4 |
| Profit & loss | 284.1 | 324.7 | 375.7 |
| Surplus | 314.5 | 360.1 | 430.1 |
| Sales | 584.0 | 601.0 | 690.0 |
| Net profit (pre-tax) | 60.0 | 75.6 | 105.0 |
| after depreciation | 6.5 | 6.5 | 6.0 |
| after directors' remuneration | 35.0 | 40.0 | 42.0 |
| Less tax | 30.0 | 35.0 | 54.0 |
| Net profit after tax | 30.0 | 40.6 | 51.0 |

As might be expected, the bank account had worked well. In
September 1978 the company's overdraft limit was £80,000 secured
by the freehold deeds of the factory valued at £70,000 in April 1978.

The overall statistics were as follows:

| (All figures in '000s) | 1975 | 1976 | 1977 | 1978 (to June) |
|---|---|---|---|---|
| Turnover | 600.0 | 680.0 | 826.0 | 550.0 |
| Average balance | 33.0 cr | 48.0 cr | 20.0 cr | 2.0 cr |
| Range: Worst | 2.0 cr | 8.0 cr | 37.0 dr | 60.0 dr |
| Best | 66.0 cr | 102.0 cr | 52.0 cr | 35.0 cr |

The Directors were honest and hard working. They were capable engineers manufacturing a quality product which enjoyed a good position in the market. The bank held the business in high esteem. But problems had arisen inside the company without anyone connected with it being aware of them. An in-depth survey conducted in September 1978[3] revealed the following problems:

**a.** A serious decline in profitability due to an undetected rise in raw material prices and overheads.

**b.** A liquidity problem caused by production delays, overstocking and a long lag in the receipt of funds from trade debtors overseas.

**c.** Inadequate control of costs, particularly non-productive labour time.

**d.** An almost total absence of up-to-date management information.

Some of these difficulties will be examined in more detail in later chapters; the point to be made at this stage is that traditional tools provided no assistance in identifying and remedying the company's problems. For such help we must enlist the aid of management accounting.

## References and notes

[1] Sizer, J.: *An Insight into Management Accounting.* Penguin, 1974.
[2] Ray, G. and Smith, J.: *Hardy Heating Co. Ltd: text and cases in management accounting.* Midland Consultant Publications, 1974.
[3] This is, of course, not the actual date of the survey. The timescale of this case study has been altered to suit the publication of this book.

## Further reading

As a relatively easy introduction to management accounting my own preference is:
Harper, W.M.: *Management Accounting.* 2nd ed. Macdonald and Evans, 1977.

CHAPTER 4

# The Start of the Planning Process

## 4.1. THE NEED FOR OBJECTIVES

The starting point for a plan which is to have any chance of success is the establishment of corporate objectives. This is not an easy area, and I have been tempted to follow the route of several books on management accounting by leaving the reader to search elsewhere for any pointers on the subject. But a few words are essential if for no other reason than the fact that a banker is well placed to make occasional suggestions to his corporate customers about the future path of their business. He is close enough to the company to appreciate its potential yet sufficiently removed for his vision to be unimpaired by the day-to-day operational problems which cloud the horizon for almost every business manager. It is not something to be discussed on every visit, or even referred to directly at all. Better to talk one's way around the proprietor's/director's hopes and aspirations in general terms and then provide a few hints on those areas of a company's performance which are of the greatest importance.

This chapter will not be spiced with heavy doses of technical terms or jargon. The smaller business is not normally knowingly concerned with 'capability profiles' or 'strategic planning', but requires a little more of its managers than that they should continually and exclusively be attempting to solve yesterday's problems. Some forward planning seems essential if a business is not to miss the good opportunities which present themselves from time to time or risk wasting effort and money exploring every single new avenue regardless of the logic, or lack of it, in placing them alongside the company's mainstream activities. We are looking for a means to show the managing director of a small firm that increasing sales might not be the only objective to aim for, or the business proprietor who is only seeking a quiet life in his country cottage that there is no inalienable rule for his small engineering shop to go on producing profits at a good rate merely because it has always done so in the past.

Any system or procedure that seeks to improve the ability of a business to plan and control its operations more effectively will stand little chance of success unless the company has clearly established its aims. There should be a facility to compare actual results with the figures management is hoping to achieve. A business must plan to a purpose; it should have a destination of some kind in mind.

## 4.2.  HOW SHOULD OBJECTIVES BE SET?

With so many differing views on the subject of corporate objectives provided by the writers of the past few decades, it can be difficult for a banker to know what type of lead to provide. So far as the smaller business is concerned, I prefer the idea expressed by a number of authors that companies do not have objectives, only the individuals who run them do. Almost every major decision taken by a smaller firm will – to a greater or lesser extent – be a reflection of the personal ambitions of the business manager concerned.

How then can a banker assist in the setting of objectives, bearing in mind the individual nature of most business enterprises and the people who run them? To my mind help can be provided in three main ways:

**a.** First, by stressing that the setting of the overall aims of an enterprise must be the responsibility of top management. It is their prime task and one they cannot delegate. It is not an easy job and may well require much time and thought. In the 1960s the management of Avis deliberated for six months before deciding on one objective: 'It took us six months to define one objective – which turned out to be, "we want to become the fastest-growing company with the highest profit margins in the business of renting and leasing vehicles without drivers" '.[1] But the effort was worthwhile. It forced them to reconsider proposed acquisitions outside this definition and to shed subsidiaries which acted as minor dams to the mainstream of their operations: 'This let us put the blinders on ourselves and stop considering the acquisition of related businesses like motels, hotels, airlines, and travel agencies. It also showed us that we had to get rid of some limousine and sightseeing companies that we already owned'.[2]

**b.** Secondly, by emphasising that a company's aims should attempt to follow certain basic rules. These are that objectives should be:

– **Quantified:** vague aims, such as 'a large increase in turnover', 'a much improved profitability', 'an increasing market share', do not provide a clearly defined path for a business. Precise objectives enable management to calculate the extent of improvements to be made if the business is moving off course.

– **Ambitious:** management should aim to utilise the resources at its disposal to the full; they should stretch themselves and their materials. Even a seemingly unambitious target, such as 'to maintain the present level of sales', can provide a sufficient challenge in an industry where demand is declining.

– **Attainable:** targets should be set to be reached, however ambitiously they are determined. They must take account of the company's strengths and weaknesses and the environment in which it operates. A business should use all its resources to achieve its targets and make certain that its information system is a help in this connection rather than a pure cost serving no useful purpose.

– **Flexible:** this is not meant to suggest that aims should be altered at regular intervals as it becomes apparent that the business is not achieving the original objectives, but that the management should not adhere slavishly to targets that have been rendered obsolete by changing circumstances. Objectives should have an air of permanence but should not be enshrined as an unchanging idol to be placed in the boardroom alongside the portrait of the founder.

– **Appropriate:** corporate objectives should be bespoke; carefully tailored to fit the real needs and aspirations of a business.

**c.** Last, but most important, objectives must concentrate on the key items which contribute to the building of a successful business. Often when I have held a seminar on the subject matter covered in this book I have asked the participants for an off-the-cuff list of the ingredients that they think make up corporate success. Usually a long list is produced which includes such areas as managerial flair, saleable products, good labour relations (often thought synonymous with a non-union operation, although this is rarely the case in practice), adequate productive capacity, an easy life and so on. Obviously there is no one universal package of aims which will fit all, or more than a few, sets of circumstances but it is difficult to envisage a situation where a firm should not set precise and quantifiable objectives in at least one of these areas:

> – Profitability (however measured).
> – Liquidity.
> – Product mix.
> – Market position.
> – Productivity.

It is also difficult to escape the conclusion that two of these areas are of such supreme importance that if they are not properly planned and controlled it is virtually impossible for a business to survive for any length of time and the quality of the other ingredients becomes of academic interest. These two factors are *profitability* and *liquidity*, and much of what follows in the remainder of this book is concerned with their planning and control. All bankers recognise that there is often no practical relationship between profits earned and the cash resources of a business, and that the two needs are commonly in conflict. 'Profit is an opinion, but cash is a fact' is an often-expressed thought in banking circles. But businessmen fail to distinguish between the two with a frightening regularity, frequently with disastrous results. There have been numerous cases over the past few years of companies, by no means solely at the smaller end of the scale, failing because they were so intent on achieving longer term profitability that they ignored the need for adequate liquidity. Equally frequently the need to meet pressing demands for cash has forced businesses to forego profits through selling their goods and services to the first willing buyer who was not demanding credit terms.

There is also often some confusion between the words profit and profitability. The first is an *absolute* measure and the second a *relative* one. A simple example will serve to illustrate the point:

---

**(All figures in '000s)**

|  | Year 1 | Year 2 |
|---|---|---|
| Sales | 100.0 | 200.0 |
| Direct labour | 20.0 | 40.0 |
| Direct materials | 40.0 | 80.0 |
| Overheads | 30.0 | 65.0 |
| Profit | 10.0 | 15.0 |
| Profitability $\left[\dfrac{\text{Profit}}{\text{Sales}} \times 100\right]$ | 10% | 7.5% |

---

This business has increased its profits over the period in absolute terms by £5,000, but its profitability – measured in this case by relating profits to sales – has decreased by 25 per cent (a commonly encountered alternative method of assessing profitability is to relate net profits to capital employed). This reduction may not represent a problem for the business; it all depends on its aims and the yardsticks it wishes to use in evaluating corporate success.

Management accounting can provide invaluable help in the planning and control of profitability and liquidity. If, as I believe to be the position, these two components are of such crucial importance, then the case for a good working knowledge of the subject for bankers and their customers is irrefutable. But it must be remembered that it is not the role of management accounting to set objectives; its place is to help achieve them.

## 4.3. OBJECTIVES IN PRACTICE

The directors of *XL Engineering* had never attempted to quantify their objectives beyond expressing a general desire to build a sound expanding company that would provide for their families and children in the future. Somewhat less openly but with equal enthusiasm they expressed a desire 'to pay the tax man as little as possible' – an attainable and flexible aim, but hardly ambitious!

After a good deal of discussion during which the directors initially expressed considerable scepticism it was agreed that objectives would be established by using ratios[3] for the following:

| | |
|---|---|
| Profitability | 1. Net profit/Sales. |
| | 2. Net profit/Capital employed. |
| | 3. Sales/Capital employed. |
| Liquidity | 4. Current assets/Current liabilities. |
| | 5. Quick assets/Current liabilities. |

It was felt that this programme for 'management by objectives' would provide a much clearer path on which to control the future of the business and, by establishing clear targets, help the directors in setting priorities.

'*The Corporate Report*', a discussion paper produced for the Accounting Standards Committee,[4] has much to say on the subject of business objectives. The results of a commissioned survey also make interesting reading: 58 per cent of the companies responding to the survey stated that their primary objective related to profit (significantly a further 10 per cent put their prime aim as survival), and it is difficult to avoid the contention that profit will always be a priority area – 'whatever its other functions, a company exists to make money for its owners, and its future is guaranteed or jeopardised according to the satisfaction, or lack of it, that the shareholders exhibit regarding its performance on their behalf'.[5]

I make no apology for reproducing one reply to the survey in full:

'Our purpose in business is to create wealth, to make money. For this to be possible we must please our customers and enjoy the confidence of our shareholders and employees. We must make good profits, so that after providing for taxes and dividends (and in present conditions financing inflation) there is available enough money to keep our factories and equipment modern and to enable us to grow in strength and maintain or improve our market position. We endeavour to provide good, satisfying employment to our people. Creating wealth and building a better company is our contribution to better standards of living.'

Contrast this with other replies: 'To give the best possible service' and 'To provide a service to customers which is better than that of our competitors', and the value of good objectives is vividly demonstrated.

### References and notes

[1] Townsend, R.: *Up the Organisation*. Michael Joseph, 1970.
[2] *Ibid.*
[3] These ratios are more fully explained in Chapter 13.
[4] Published by The Institute of Chartered Accountants in England and Wales, 1975.
[3] Samuels, J.M. and Wilkes, F.M.: *Management of Company Finance*. 2nd ed. Nelson, 1975.

### Further reading

Argenti, J.: *Corporate Planning, a practical guide*. Allen and Unwin, 1968.

CHAPTER 5

# Costing

## 5.1. INTRODUCTION – A DISCUSSION

The logic of following on the need for corporate objectives with a chapter on costing and cost systems may not be immediately apparent. But if there is a recognisable base point for management accounting, then it is costing; it provides the backbone of the subject.

It is a vast topic and no attempt will be made to cover the entire field. I shall concentrate on:
– The need for a costing system.
– The techniques employed, outlining their strengths and weaknesses.
– The value of an understanding of costing to the lending banker.

It is impossible to overstress the importance of costing, yet it is an area where misconceptions and muddled thinking are the rule rather than the exception. No other area provided such fruitful pastures for my bank's Business Advisory Service; time and again smaller businesses were found to lack both a basic understanding of the way in which costs accrue and the ability to recover them fully. There must be innumerable cases of managers of firms rushing into their banks to request a higher facility to meet pressing creditors, with the explanation that the difficulty is entirely the fault of slow-paying debtors, when in reality the problem started many months previously through inadequacies in their own costing systems. An appreciation of the basic techniques involved would contribute more to company success than any other area of management accounting.

Although the subject is a complex one in its totality, not all problems are difficult to spot and remedy: the business that appeared to maintain a sophisticated costing system, showing figures calculated to four decimal places, which completely overlooked the need to include direct labour costs, and the steel fabricating company using a price list for steel sections that was two months out of date at the time it submitted its tenders, are examples of two firms in this category.

## 5.2. WHAT IS THE COST?

This seemingly simple question immediately opens up one large area of difficulty: 'The everyday words "cost" and "costing" cause more confused thinking and wrong decisions than any of the complex phrases like discounted cash flow, exponential smoothing, regression analysis, systems thinking and the other sophisticated techniques'.[1]

The banner headline in a newspaper 'Strike costs British Steel £10m' is open to many interpretations. Does it represent the total amount of lost turnover? Is it expected profit which will now be unrealised? Or is it increased overheads caused by deteriorating stocks and wastage? Each will produce very different answers. To the person buying a motor car the cost is the amount he pays the garage. The garage proprietor thinks of his cost as the price he pays the distributor, who in turn regards his cost as the amount due to the manufacturer. The manufacturer will probably use the term to mean the figure at the foot of his cost or estimating schedule. This figure, often shown to indicate a degree of accuracy it can never possess, has frequently been calculated using a number of subjective judgements and broad estimates that bear little relation to the actual costs incurred in the production of the article.

There is, then, no such thing as *the* cost of an article or service, only *a* cost which will vary according to the relative position in the business cycle of the person using the figure and the validity of the interpretations he has made in its calculation. The pen which I am using to write this has no absolute cost but a number of costs, and the figure that is most open to doubt and uncertainty is the estimated manufacturing cost calculated by the producer.

## 5.3. WHY COST?

As with all forms of management accounting, cost information should only be produced if it serves a useful purpose. A manager of a smaller business will probably say he produces costing figures 'to help me fix prices', ignoring the other important uses for the information and being unaware of the limitations of the final result. In a large company the army of cost accountants and clerks who have been spending the bulk of their time over the last few months deciding whether or not it is equitable for Product A to bear 2.3 per cent of the cost of the night watchman may be reluctant to call a temporary halt to their labours to query the meaning of the figures or their value to management.

There are three main uses for costing information; all have some value:

**a. To provide an estimated cost for a product both in its finished state and as work-in-progress.** This aids price setting because no business normally wishes to fix selling prices below its costs (the exceptions to this rule and the idea that costing information is merely an aid to pricing rather than its sole determinant are discussed in the next chapter) and it may also assign a value to goods held in stock.

We shall see in a moment that there are serious difficulties associated with this concept, particularly in the calculation of the proportion of overheads to be carried by a product or process.

**b. To aid control.** Business managers need to decide before the event what costs ought to be; this enables them to compare actual with estimated performance. This is a vital function and one the company with none of the basic information is powerless to carry out. The essence of cost control is establishing plans, monitoring actual results, examining the variances and taking action to remedy a situation where necessary.

A small jobbing builder in the West Country never compared actual labour hours with targets set at the estimating stage. The result – losses were incurred on many contracts where jobs took longer than expected and similar work was taken on at an identical price because the company remained in blissful ignorance of the true position. Conversely, many tenders were not accepted by potential customers because an overestimation of labour cost not identified on earlier jobs led to unattractive prices in the market place.

**c. As an aid to decision making.** The essential task of a company manager is to choose between alternative uses for the scarce resources placed at his disposal now and in the future and to assign priorities. There are many areas of decision making where the right type of costing information is of enormous value – for example, investing in capital equipment; changing the volume of output; making or buying; altering the product mix or introducing a new product.

This use is particularly important where there is a significant alteration in the cost structure of a business. For example, I visited a firm in the West Indies which had operated very successfully for several years in the garage of the owner, who viewed it as a spare-time occupation to supplement his normal income. The low-priced product had found a gap in the market, sales had increased rapidly and on the strength of the obvious potential which existed the decision was taken to move the manufacturing process to a large, new factory. The result was disastrous. Although sales leapt as production caught up with the latent demand, the increase was not sufficient to carry the burden of the new level of overheads. Profits were soon turned into losses which could only be financed from the liquid surplus of the business. The strain on current resources quickly forced it into liquidation. A simple forecast of the likely increases in costs resulting from the expanded operation would have saved much misery.

## 5.4. CLASSIFICATION OF COSTS

These three uses cannot be satisfied with costing information produced to a common format. There are a number of ways of classifying costs to make the figures more meaningful; the method chosen will be determined by the purpose for which they are required:

**a. By type of expense** – materials, labour and other expenses. This classification separates those costs which are easily identified with a product from those which are not. 'Direct' costs, such as raw materials forming part of the finished article or labour employed on the production process, are distinguished from 'indirect' costs, such as rates, depreciation and maintenance personnel. The total of all direct items is known as the 'prime cost', and the remaining costs when lumped together are called the 'overheads'.

**b. By function** – production, administration, selling, distribution, etc. This is the method commonly used in the audited accounts.

**c. By location** – departments, product ranges and cost centres. In this classification the accountant draws a distinction between costs which can be 'allocated', that is, attributed in total easily and directly to the area in which they are incurred, and costs which can only be 'apportioned', that is, those that cannot be applied directly to departments or cost centres and must be shared among various locations on some arbitrary basis.

An example of allocation might be power costs where the usage of machines in various areas of the factory can easily be identified. Conversely, the cost of, for example, the managing director's car can often only be apportioned using less than precise rules of thumb.

**d. By relationship to changes in activity.** This method segregates costs into those that vary in proportion to changes in the level of activity, known as 'variable' costs, and those that remain unaltered regardless of fluctuations in activity which are known as 'fixed' costs.

For the purposes of this book, I shall regard all direct costs as being variable and all indirect costs as fixed. This is an oversimplification which would meet with little approval from many cost accountants, but it will, I hope, make what follows more comprehensible.

Some of these cost classifications will help us to examine the main costing methods more closely.

## 5.5. METHODS OF COSTING

### a. Absorption costing

This is by far the most commonly used costing method. For many businesses it is the only method with which they are familiar. At first glance it may seem to be the only safe way of conducting a business but there are often major problems surrounding the calculations, particularly those concerning the recovery of indirect costs.

The system is based on the idea that all the costs of operating a business should be charged in some way to a product or a range of products, a process or a cost unit. The product is said to 'absorb' its proportion of the total costs. As a procedure it is fraught with difficulties and involves many problems of interpretation and analysis. These can best be illustrated by returning to the actual case mentioned in Chapter 3: *XL Engineering Co. Ltd.*

The company has been invited to submit a tender for a section of a steel bridge, and a full set of drawings has been supplied.

The manager responsible for estimating looks first at *direct materials* and decides how much is required in volume terms; these quantities are then converted into costs. This sounds a simple step, but there are pitfalls in many industries:

i In estimating quantity, an allowance may be required for:
– Scrap and wastage. In a number of companies this may not be a serious problem. Or it may be merely a convenient excuse for inefficiency given by managers who have no knowledge of the true position. In others, however, scrap and wastage can be a source of heavy, unrecouped cost. (A furniture manufacturer was unaware that the level of scrap wood had increased from 10 per cent to 30 per cent following the installation of a mechanised saw which automatically rejected any piece of timber containing the slightest imperfec-

tion. As wood accounted for 35 per cent of total costs the oversight proved to be an expensive one.)
– 'Shrinkage'. Pilferage is much more prevalent than most managers believe and in some industries it is rife. It will often be the case that the expense of continually policing stocks will be more than the possible savings, but any firm wishing to maintain its profit margins must at least make itself aware of the quantity and value of materials disappearing through the back door. (Excessive scrap and shrinkage indicate the need for an effective system of stock control and this will be examined in Chapter 12.)
*ii* In estimating price, consideration must be given to:
– Impending price changes. Many businesses fail to make the relatively undemanding effort required to forecast future price levels. There is little point in using the current price for steel in an estimate of the sort being compiled by *XL Engineering* if the actual purchase order will not be placed until many months later when the fate of the tender is known.
– Purchasing policy. Some businesses anticipate price increases by buying forward. This is a sound policy where the contract is 'in the bag', but many forget to include in their estimates the high cost inherent in holding this stock until it is required.
– Pricing materials issued from stock. This is an area where misunderstandings are commonplace both within businesses and outside them. Raw materials and partly finished goods are often held in stock at a figure which does not reflect their value to the business or their current cost. The manner in which the difference should be allowed for is a question for managerial judgement which we shall examine in more detail later; the point to be made at this juncture is that its existence should not escape the attention of the estimating manager.
– Impact on working capital. The manufacturing process must be financed from the moment the first nut and bolt are purchased until the time when payment is received from the customer. Such finance costs money: the higher the initial outlay on raw materials and the longer the period of manufacturing, the greater the cost.

Next the company examines *direct labour costs*. As before, the first step is to produce a volume measurement – normally total hours required to complete – which is converted into a monetary value. This poses more problems than the assessment of direct materials, the main areas of difficulty being:
*i* Time required – it can prove inordinately difficult to produce an

accurate estimate of the number of hours required for a job, particularly if the costing system has not been used for control purposes in the past.

*ii* Calculating 'true' labour cost – many figures produced are wildly inaccurate because no account is taken of full labour costs, total available working hours or labour efficiency. An eminent writer on company success, Peter Drucker, has said '. . . the hidden costs of any activity are always much greater than anybody assumes or than any accounting system shows. To keep a man on the payroll always costs at least three times his wage or salary. He needs space to work in, heat, light and a locker in the washroom. He needs materials to work with, supplies, a telephone, and so on. He needs a supervisor. In a hundred hidden ways he creates costs'.[2]

Examining the costs that an accounting system can record:

| | | | |
|---|---|---|---|
| Annual wage<br>(£1.44 per hour based on<br>52 weeks of 40 hours) | | £3,000 | |
| National insurance<br>(employer's share) | | 250 | |
| Additional benefits, say, | | 35 | |
| Total wage cost  (A) | | £3,285 | Ideally, figures should take<br>account of future rises. |
| Annual hours available | | 2,080 | |
| Less: Sickness | 80 | | |
| Holidays | 120 | | |
| Relaxation | 235 | 435 | |
| Available working hours (B) | | 1,645 | |

Hourly rate (C)

$$= \frac{A}{B} \qquad £2$$

Labour efficiency — A factor that must be considered. There is no point in seeking to recover labour costs on hours that are nonproductive (unless the customer pays for this time, as is often the case with a garage business). A low efficiency does not necessarily imply a poor work force; it can arise for reasons beyond the control of labour, e.g. poor production control, changes in product mix, staff training. In practice, a good costing system can aid the measurement of this figure.

Assume rate 80%

Actual cost

$$= \frac{C}{80\%} \qquad £2.50 \text{ Contrast with basic hourly rate of £1.44.}$$

It is this figure of £2.50 which will be multiplied by the estimated labour hours to produce an amount for total labour cost. Any error in the rate will, therefore, cause large distortions in the estimated total cost of constructing the steel section. It should be noted that even with the adjustments shown above no allowance has been made for overtime payments, incentive schemes or the use of different grades of labour on parts of the job.

With these estimates completed, a figure for prime cost has been produced, that is a total for all expected direct costs. Next the estimating manager turns his attention to the recovery of *overheads*. The difficulties encountered in completing figures thus far are small in comparison with those associated with the reclamation of overheads. Most of the shortcomings of absorption costing stem from the problems that follow:

*i* The ascertainment of overhead costs – it is an almost unbelievable fact that many firms do not bother with this step. They simply use a recovery rate that they feel is right, perhaps because they half heard a whisper several years ago that one of their competitors down the road was using a similar figure. It is, however, usually an easy task to obtain historical information from the last audited accounts and only slightly more difficult (and much more desirable) to forecast likely costs as they will arise when the product is made.

*ii* The method of recovery – having calculated the total amount to be recovered, a method must be found to attach a part of the total to a product. There are a number of acceptable methods in common use, one of the most frequently encountered being a percentage on direct labour hours or costs. The rules governing the choice are few, but very important; the basis should be an equitable one and it should be related to the occurrence of the overheads.

One company I visited recovered overheads by the addition of a set percentage to direct labour cost which accounted for only 6 per cent of sales revenue – this against a figure of nearly 60 per cent for direct materials to sales. Since direct labour cost was virtually unrelated to the incidence of overheads, there was no possible logic in this system and it caused large distortions to appear in the company's prices for small differences in the labour cost content.

*iii* The level of activity – having ascertained the actual or projected level of total overheads and having decided that the best method of recovery is, say, on direct labour hours, *XL Engineering* need to produce a figure for the total of that activity available during the relevant period. This is not easy; if they decide to take a longer-term view (in the costing context) by forecasting total labour hours for one year ahead and the actual hours fall below the figure expected, then the result will be an underrecovery of overheads; in turn producing a lower profit or a loss. On the other hand, if total labour hours for the year are higher than expected, the company will overrecover; excellent news at first glance, but it may mean that its products have been priced more highly than they might otherwise have been and volume may suffer.

The last step in the estimating process is to add an amount for profit. The completed calculation could look like this:

## XL Engineering

*Cost estimate*

Tender 950

|  | £ |  |
|---|---|---|
| Direct materials | 3,500 | Obtained from breakdown of drawing |
| Direct labour | 2,500 | 1,000 hours at a 'true' rate of £2.50 per hour |
| Prime cost | 6,000 |  |
| Overheads |  | Total projected overheads for year = £105,000. Total projected available labour hours = 1,645 x 20 men = 32,900. But 80% efficiency, so = 26,320. Therefore, recovery rate per labour hour = $\frac{105,000}{26,320}$ Say, = £4 per hour |
| Therefore, amount to be recovered on this job | 4,000 | (£4 x 1,000) |
| Total cost | 10,000 |  |
| Profit @ 25% | 2,500 |  |
| Suggested price | 12,500 |  |

A simple point, but one worth mentioning because so many businesses get it wrong: a profit mark up of 25 per cent does not result in an equivalent net profit percentage; the figure reduces to 20 per cent:

$$\text{Net Profit \%} = \frac{\text{Net Profit}}{\text{Sales}} \times 100 = \frac{2,500 \times 100}{12,500} = 20\%$$

The choice of a basis for recovering overheads was relatively easy for the managers of *XL Engineering;* a set percentage of all overheads could be added to the prime cost of all products in a comparatively fair way. In many companies the position is more complicated because all products do not follow identical routes through the factory and in these circumstances it is obviously inequitable to attach similar proportions of all overheads to each product. For example, in a textile company producing a wide range of fabrics many cloths will bypass expensive machines used for specialised work; it would be unfair for these products to carry the same proportion of, say, depreciation as those passing through all spheres of operation. Similarly, in a hotel business it can be very difficult to decide how much of the items of overhead should be apportioned between the restaurant and the letting of rooms. There is no precise answer to these problems; they are matters for individual judgement.

Absorption costing, then, can provide some assistance, albeit with considerable imperfections, in satisfying the first purpose of a costing system – the ascertainment of an estimated cost of a product or service. It is little help with the remainder. The control of costs is more appropriately the province of standard costing, whilst an understanding of marginal costing is invaluable for decision making.

## b. Standard costing

This is the pre-eminent method for cost control, but it is a detailed subject in its entirety and a full explanation must be beyond the aims of this book. It consists of establishing target costs (standards) in terms of both quantity and price, monitoring actual results against those forecast, analysing the variances and taking action in the light of the information revealed. Prompt information is produced for executive decisions, and managerial time is saved because only those variances which are significant require attention.

On the minus side, the system is often complex and difficult to install, calls for time-consuming adjustments during periods of high inflation and is frequently not fully understood by managers responsible for its smooth functioning.

## c. Marginal costing

Marginal costing is primarily an aid to decision making. It is not a substitute for other forms of costing, but complementary to them.

With absorption costing, the difficulties encountered in recovering overheads lead to faulty information for managers. The system also has the major weakness of not providing information on how costs will move as a result of changing business structures. Marginal costing avoids these inadequacies by concentrating on the margin between sales revenue and variable costs. The difference is known as the *contribution* and it represents the amount available to meet overheads and provide a profit.

By way of illustration, a marginal costing approach to the estimating schedule for *XL Engineering* would alter the structure of the figures:

|  | £ |
|---|---|
| Sales | 12,500 |
| Direct materials | 3,500 |
| Direct labour | 2,500 |
| Total variable cost | 6,000 |
| Contribution | 6,500 |

Nothing magical has been seen thus far, as the contribution of £6,500 is merely the total of overheads (£4,000) and profit (£2,500) produced in the earlier calculation.

The real value becomes more apparent when, for example, three different products are compared, using first an absorption and then a marginal approach to the costs:

**Absorption costing**

|  | Product A £ | Product B £ | Product C £ | Total £ |
|---|---|---|---|---|
| Sales | 1,000 | 1,000 | 500 | 2,500 |
| Materials | 600 | 300 | 300 | 1,200 |
| Wages | 100 | 300 | 100 | 500 |
| Overheads | 150 | 300 | 150 | 600 |
| Total costs | 850 | 900 | 550 | 2,300 |
| Profit | 150 | 100 |  | 200 (net) |
| Loss |  |  | 50 |  |

From this it appears that Product A is more profitable than Product B, and that Product C is making a loss. In the absence of mitigating circumstances, many firms would discontinue production of C and concentrate their resources on the two remaining products which are profitable.

But this argument is based on a fallacy for, if product C is dropped, overheads will, by definition, continue to run at the same level as previously and products A and B will be forced to carry the £150 previously borne by C. Unless A and B can produce a greater contribution from the increased resources at their disposal, and this is often unlikely to happen in practice, then the net effect is a reduced profit of £100 for the business (£250–£150).

A marginal cost approach recognises this dilemma:

Marginal costing

|  | Product A | Product B | Product C | Total |
|---|---|---|---|---|
|  | £ | £ | £ | £ |
| Sales | 1,000 | 1,000 | 500 | 2,500 |
| Materials | 600 | 300 | 300 | 1,200 |
| Wages | 100 | 300 | 100 | 500 |
| Total variable costs | 700 | 600 | 400 | 1,700 |
| Contribution | 300 | 400 | 100 | 800 |
| Fixed costs |  |  |  | 600 |
| Profit |  |  |  | 200 |

This method enables it to be clearly seen that C is making a contribution to profits and overheads of £100 which would be lost if it ceased to be manufactured. Interestingly, B is making a larger contribution than A, although total sales are the same and A appeared to be more profitable on an absorption basis.

Marginal costing is a strong weapon that can be used over a wide range of decisions – 'It is a powerful tool for increasing profits through improving the product mix. It is invaluable in making decisions about whether to make-in or buy-out. It is a sound basis for comparing different methods of manufacture'.[3] To take one simple case: a business turns aside a job which pays £4.50 per labour hour because the proprietor has calculated that his full costing rate is £5 per hour including variable costs of £3 per hour; *in the absence of more profitable work* this will often not make sense since the job offered would contribute £1.50 per hour to overheads. Yet this folly is perpetrated many times every day in the business world.

However, marginal costing must be used with care. It will not save a product that no longer has a market or a company that is badly managed. All too often it is used in dire circumstances that it can only exacerbate – to boost ailing sales by selling all products over a long period at prices fractionally in excess of variable costs. This is the road to disaster. Marginal costing relies on strong central control to ensure that sufficient contribution is being generated over the whole product range to cover overheads and make a profit.

## 5.6. IMPLICATIONS FOR BANKERS

### a. Profitability

A number of the possible effects of a poor approach to costing have already been brought out. Most important of all, any business failing to recoup its overheads because of an inadequate recovery rate will not be making a profit. Many businesses aim for a mark up of, say, 20 per cent on their costs and yet their accounts reveal a small net profit of perhaps 3 per cent on sales; frequently no sound explanation of the root cause of the disparity can be given and bankers hear excuses which make sense to the businessman but have little foundation in reality – 'problems in setting up a new machine' or 'of course, it's all made up in the stock figure'.

Sometimes a system which works successfully when it is first introduced will be rendered obsolete by changing circumstances. If the managers of *XL Engineering* fail to adjust their recovery rate for two years (a not uncommon feature of costing in small businesses) and in that time materials have increased by 20 per cent, labour by 10 per cent and overheads by 30 per cent, then an estimate for a similar job to tender 950 will be produced as follows:

|  | £ |  |
|---|---|---|
| Direct materials | 4,200 | Rise of 20% (detected) |
| Direct labour | 2,750 | Rise of 10% (detected) |
| Prime cost | 6,950 |  |
| Overheads | 4,000 | £4 per labour hour (as previously) |
| Total cost | 10,950 |  |
| Profit (@ 25%) | 2,740 |  |
| Suggested price | 13,690 |  |

But overheads have actually moved ahead by 30 per cent, so the allocated cost should be £4,000 + 30 per cent = £5,200, giving:

|  | £ |  |
|---|---|---|
| Prime cost | 6,950 | As above |
| Overheads | 5,200 |  |
| Total cost | 12,150 |  |

The result is a reduced profit of £1,540: a reduction of over 40 per cent in the amount expected by the company. With different figures the end position could easily have been a loss.

## b. Liquidity

Effects on liquidity can be the most frightening aspect of inadequacies in costing systems because they often remain undetected in many businesses until it is too late. In the last example, *XL Engineering* believe they have recovered £10,950 on their costs when cash is received for the goods and naturally they hope that this will enable them to finance a further similar project. In the days of stable prices this would have been the case and even today the managers of the company do not feel unduly concerned, reasoning that even if all costs increase by a further 20 per cent they have a positive cash flow from the profit of £2,740 on their last job to provide the liquid funds they need to finance the current project:

|  | £ |  |
|---|---|---|
| Direct materials | 5,040 | + 20% (detected) |
| Direct labour | 3,300 | + 20% (detected) |
| Prime cost | 8,340 |  |
| Overheads | 4,000 | £4 per labour hour (company still using old rate) |
| Total cost | 12,340 |  |

They believe that the total revenue of £13,690 they received previously will enable them to cope with this increased level of costs without the need to raise finance outside the business, but in reality the position is:

|  | £ |  |
|---|---|---|
| Prime cost | 8,340 |  |
| Overheads | 6,240 | £5,200 + 20% |
| Total cost | 14,580 |  |

This calculation produces a shortfall of £890 in the cash required to finance the new job. If repeated many times across the company's product range this situation would probably raise problems at any time even with a good information system; it becomes critical when the managers do not know it exists until it is too late in the conditions of the present day.

## c. Stock

Conventional accounting principles state that stock should generally be valued at the lower of cost or net realisable value and that on no account should any element of profit be included.[4] This is a sensible and prudent view – but what is the cost, bearing in mind the difficulties and inconsistencies which exist in its determination?

The figures for raw materials, work-in-progress and finished goods in a balance sheet and trading account can rarely have the precise values that bankers would like to attribute to them, and this completely ignores the added complication of 'adjustments' for tax purposes. Much depends on the costing system and stock policy of the company concerned, and the following examples illustrate some of the differences that arise in practice.

*i* Costs included in valuations. Three companies have a turnover of £1m per annum. They all maintain a reasonably constant and similar product mix and on average their sales revenue total is made up of:

|  | £ |
|---|---|
| Direct materials | 200,000 (20%) |
| Direct labour | 300,000 (30%) |
| Other direct expenses | 100,000 (10%) |
| Overheads | 300,000 (30%) |
| Profit | 100,000 (10%) |

At the end of their financial year, which falls on the same day, they all have £300,000 of stock remaining *at selling price* composed of identical units. A Company never includes more than basic raw materials in its valuations. B Company includes 50 per cent of labour cost in work-in-progress and 100 per cent in finished goods, whilst C Company uses the same basis as B, but adds on 50 per cent of direct expenses for work-in-progress valuations and 100 per cent for completed work. Assuming the three types of stock are equally divided this produces the following year-end valuations:

|  | Finished goods | Work-in-progress | Raw materials | Total |
|---|---|---|---|---|
|  | £ | £ | £ | £ |
| A  Company | 20,000 | 20,000 | 20,000 | 60,000 |
| B  Company | 50,000 | 35,000 | 20,000 | 105,000 |
| C  Company | 60,000 | 40,000 | 20,000 | 120,000 |

C appears to be carrying twice as much stock as A, although in reality we have said that the units are identical for all three businesses. This will have the dual effect of increasing the assets in C's balance sheet and pushing up reported profit.[5]

*ii* Valuing material issues. The method used to value materials issued from stores has a significant effect on stock values and therefore on recorded profit. The records of R Company and S Company are:

---

*Record of stock purchased — common to R  Co. and S  Co.*

| Date | Units purchased | Purchase price per unit | Units issued |
|------|-----------------|-------------------------|--------------|
| 1 January | 2,000 | £100 | |
| 10 March | 1,500 | £150 | |
| 20 June | | | 1,000 |
| 1 September | | | 1,300 |
| 21 October | 800 | £200 | |
| 15 December | | | 1,000 |

*Consumed stock — charge to profit and loss account/basis of valuation*

| Units issued | R  Co. FIFO (First in, first out) | | S  Co. LIFO (Last in, first out) | |
|------|----------|-----------------|----------|-----------------|
| 1,000 | £100,000 | (1,000 x £100) | £150,000 | (1,000 x £150) |
| 1,300 | £145,000 | (1,000 x £100) (300 x £150) | £155,000 | (500 x £150) (800 x £100) |
| 1,000 | £150,000 | (1,000 x £150) | £180,000 | (800 x £200) (200 x £100) |
| | £395,000 | | £485,000 | |

*Unconsumed stock — balance sheet*

| Quantity | Value R  Co. FIFO | | S  Co. LIFO | |
|----------|----------|-----------------|----------|-----------------|
| 1,000 (4,300–3,300) | £190,000 | (200 x £150) (800 x £200) | £100,000 | (1,000 x £100) |

---

There are a number of methods of valuing materials issued; the two shown here are simply intended to illustrate the large discrepancies which can arise. In this example R Company has a much lower charge to its profit and loss account than S Company and corresponding increase in the value remaining for transfer to its balance sheet, although the underlying transactions are identical for both companies.

## 5.7.  COSTING – A VITAL AREA

Many businesses ignore the problems which abound in costing, presumably in the hope that this will cause them to go away; they never do. Others often consider costing systems a luxury they cannot afford; unfortunately the reverse is the case.

Costing is a crucial ingredient in company success and bankers ignore it at their peril. 'For too long, costing has been regarded as the province of the accountant. Yet . . . it is much too important to be left to the experts. It offers a goldmine of profit opportunities for managers who are prepared to dig.'[6]

No one system of costing can be said to be the 'best' for all industries in all conditions. Businessmen should be aware of the strengths and weaknesses of the main methods described above, but unfortunately this is frequently not the case. As a generalisation it is fair to say that absorption costing has been relied upon too much by those who have not seen its faults, while the benefits of a marginal costing approach have remained a mystery to all but a few.

### References and notes

[1] Wood, E.G.: 'How to Cost'. *Management Today*, October 1973.
[2] Drucker, P.: *Managing for Results*. Pan, 1967.
[3] Wood, E.G.: *op. cit.*
[4] An exception arises with long-term contract work in progress, the treatment of which is dealt with in *Statement of Standard Accounting Practice No. 9 (SSAP 9): Stock and Work in Progress*. The Institute of Chartered Accountants in England and Wales, May 1975.
[5] This simple example is used merely to illustrate the basic point. Strictly all three companies are now at variance with SSAP 9 by excluding from their valuations part of the 'cost of conversion'. For those companies adhering to this standard similar anomalies can be illustrated using 'production overheads', the calculation of which lend themselves to differing interpretations.
[6] Wood, E.G.: *op. cit.*

CHAPTER 6

# Pricing

## 6.1. WHAT ARE THE OBJECTIVES?

Many people get the pricing decision wrong and they are not all to be found in business life. I once overheard the organiser of a local jumble sale remarking, 'we mustn't set prices too high – no point in having a lot of junk left over at the end of the day'. This is an interesting example of muddled thinking – the main aim of the event was surely not to dispose of everything because this avoided taking the unsold jumble home to clutter the loft afterwards, but to achieve the highest level of income. Once the objective has been properly thought through, the task of fixing prices comes into clearer focus: it is better to sell 600 items for 4p than 800 at 2p, and better still to sell 25 articles at £1.

The company manager will be faced with many more complexities than this of course but his first thought should always be the broad question: how do I wish our pricing policy to help in achieving our overall objectives?

## 6.2. CLASSICAL THEORIES

In my view, the first advice on pricing policy that should be given to a small businessman is to throw away any economics textbooks he may have on his shelf. The classical theories on the adjustment of prices seem to bear little relation to what actually happens at grass-roots level with the smaller firm. The type of perfect market described in most books, where the buyer is indifferent as to whom he buys from and the seller has no preference as to whom he sells to, is rarely encountered in practice. Supply and demand will always have some importance in the pricing decision, but there are often other factors of equal or greater importance. Small firms can usually adopt a more flexible approach than their larger competitors. They should be more nimble on their feet. An unusual order that may take ages to process in a big company because it runs outside of the normal pattern can often be dealt with very quickly in a small organisation more used to handling 'once-off' transactions. The smaller firm may be prepared to trade in smaller lots – I have been to several firms where this was the sole rationale behind their existence. It may carry a greater range of products and be prepared to give more personal attention and guidance to a customer. Geography may be a consideration – you may decide to buy a particular suite of furniture from a local shop merely because the thought of spending several days being pushed and prodded in the West End of London has little appeal. After-sales care has become an increasingly important determinant for many people in more recent years. And the marketing style can have a considerable impact.

All of these factors may have some effect on the price a business can charge for its products or service. Much will depend on the nature of a product and the reaction of competitors, but most of those products that are extremely price sensitive and where volume can transfer rapidly to competitors who hold their price are being produced and sold by large businesses. For example, bread is controlled by a small number of big companies who find it difficult to compete on price grounds because any cuts would quickly be matched by rivals and the net effect would merely be lower margins all round – the classic picture of an oligopoly. But small bakers can still survive and prosper by offering specialised products, i.e. home-made bread and cakes, that are capable of commanding a reasonable margin.

Economists, it seems to me, ignore the sheer perversity of the buying public who do not always favour a particular product simply because it is the cheapest available. Brand loyalty, snob value or fear of poor quality are examples of other factors which may affect the final choice. I recently had two cards pushed through my letterbox. One was nicely printed, in clear blue and white lettering and read 'The directors of . . . invite you to take advantage of their building expertise . . . our experienced staff can give expert advice and perform work at the most economic price'. The other bore amateurish printing on poor quality card and said 'For cheap rates on painting, fencing, plumbing etc., ring . . . '; note particularly the choice of adjective used to describe their respective prices. I wanted a few small jobs done around the house. I obtained quotations from each and sure enough the second firm was cheaper. But the first got the work. Why? Simply because of an unsubstantiated doubt over the quality offered by the second, brought about by the style of their advertising material.

## 6.3.  HOW SHOULD PRICES BE SET?

Smaller businesses often ask what sort of profit margins they should build into their selling prices. This is an impossible question for an outsider to answer. The only rule is that they should attempt to earn sufficient profits overall to enable the long-term aims of the business to be met. It is possible to compare net returns with industry-wide or national figures, but this is no substitute for constructive thinking on the part of individual firms.

In general, prices should be set at the highest point the market will bear for a given level of volume. This is not always easily determined and some trial and error may be necessary – this need not involve firms increasing their prices at one moment, only to be forced to reduce them the next because the market has turned against them; goods can be left at the increased recommended retail price and extensive discounts offered as an incentive to purchase.

Profit margins can sometimes be set at an enormously high level. The much publicised case of an overseas pharmaceutical company able to set margins vastly above cost because of its market leadership in certain drugs provides such an example. Often, however, the situation is short-lived; competitors are attracted to the field because of the rich pickings, and their entry brings prices down, or adverse public comment causes margins to be pruned. Companies may sometimes wish to sell at below total cost where, for example, they wish to retain the services of skilled employees who are temporarily underemployed and would be difficult to replace at a later date, or to keep valuable plant working rather than allow it to deteriorate whilst standing idle. Occasionally, similar circumstances press businesses into selling at below *variable* cost. This last situation can also arise through deliberate policy quite unforced by circumstances as, for example, when a new type of hand-razor is introduced at a very low price to promote sales of complementary razor blades on which margins are good.

## 6.4.  COMMON MISCONCEPTIONS IN PRICING

The most commonly encountered misconceptions are that:

**a.  The pricing decision is unimportant.** It sounds like stating the obvious to say that price setting is a vitally important part of any firm's responsibilities. Yet it is not treated as such by many of them; banking readers may test this by asking a representative selection of their business customers who takes the decisions on prices and how regularly they are reviewed. All too frequently selling prices are the responsibility of junior managers or subcommittees who view their task as a routine administrative function. This can be likened to asking a 10-year old boy to check the tyres on a motorcar to make sure they are roadworthy. Just as tyres are the only contact a car has with the road, and their suitability and condition often mean life or death for the driver, so selling prices are the point where a business meets its market and the response decides its success or failure.

An old-established business in the south-east of England provided a highly specialised service; one of only two firms in the country so equipped. It was unlikely that any competitors would appear to challenge their position in the market because the high degree of skill required from the manual workers could only be acquired after many years of training. Their customers were rich businessmen and wealthy landowners. On the face of it, all the ingredients for high margins were in existence, yet the firm had earned only small profits for many years and inflation had recently turned these into losses. The reason – the working directors paid no heed to prices: they took a great pride in the results of their labours and confined themselves almost exclusively to the technical aspects of the work. No one wished to change their basic way of life or condemn their desire to provide a service to a high standard, but they had to be made aware that the very survival of their business was threatened. The devotion of part of the time of one director to pricing policy ensured the continuing existence of the company.

**b. Raising prices is difficult.** Increasing prices is an area where businessmen see problems rather than opportunities: 'our customers won't stand another rise', or 'but we've just printed next year's catalogues' are typical of comments often encountered. They are, of course, arguments which may not be without some validity, but all too frequently they are used as excuses for complete inactivity.

In many businesses prices are not considered with sufficient frequency, possibly because any review these days almost invariably means an upward revision which customers and some people inside the business will find unpalatable. This is like putting off a visit to the dentist because you know that a filling is required: the longer you leave it the more painful the tooth becomes and the more extensive the final treatment.

Many managers in business are obsessed with volume. They judge success almost exclusively in terms of increased turnover and they are concerned that increased prices will send sales tumbling. This is an important consideration dealt with in Chapter 7, but managers should not be blinkered by it; profitability and liquidity are not sacrificial lambs to be slaughtered uncaringly on the altar of growth – turnover becomes unattainable and undesirable without the means to support it. In any case a number of markets are less sensitive to price than many companies believe; in the conditions of today quite large increases in both absolute and percentage terms are regularly accepted without complaint. Many consumers do not research the market looking for the bargain price as painstakingly as many producers believe; examine your last ten purchases involving an expenditure of more than, say, £25 and ask yourself how religiously you sought out the lowest price in every case.

Remember, also, that a small increase in price can produce a dramatic increase in profit. Take a company with total sales of £100,000 presently earning a net return of 10 per cent; its overall figures will be:

| | |
|---|---|
| Sales revenue | £100,000 |
| Total costs | £90,000 |
| Profit | £10,000 |

Assuming no drop in volume or increase in costs, an increase of 5 per cent in its selling prices would produce:

| | |
|---|---|
| Sales revenue | £105,000 |
| Total costs | £90,000 |
| Profit | £15,000 |

This represents a rise of 50 per cent in the net profit, ten times the percentage price increase!

At the time of writing there are legal restraints in the UK on price levels. But these do not debar all price increases or constitute a valid reason for ignoring the need for change as and when the restrictions are removed. It is a sad indictment against parts of industry that many managers have looked upon the present legislation as a convenient excuse for doing nothing. Particularly disappointing when, as Geoff Wood has commented, 'Undoubtedly, raising prices is the quickest and easiest way to increase profits, provided you can get away with it'.[1]

**c. Prices are costs plus.** It has already been said that the amount consumers are prepared to pay for a product or service is determined in the market place. In other words the final judgement rests on external influences rather than internally-produced figures of whatever type. Thus the management accountant has a limited role to play in the setting of prices; he should not dominate the decision. He can supply details of costs which will usually help in setting parameters, but this should be only one constituent of a pricing policy. Cyril Aydon makes the point fluently:

'Price-fixing is *not* a branch of costing. It is a quite separate activity. Price-fixing is a highly skilled activity for which accountants have no special aptitude or training. The price-fixer needs information about cost behaviour (from the cost office) and about customer behaviour (from the sales department), and his thinking should give equal emphasis to each. The foolish management *bases* prices on "costs". The wise management bears "costs" in mind, but is equally influenced by market considerations.'[2]

There can be little doubt that a vast number of enterprises of all sizes fail to recognise this concept and rely instead solely on the information provided by their costs. This denies them large amounts of potential profit and subjects their prices to all the inconsistencies of their costing system.

**d. Marginal costing cannot aid price setting.** Prices based on marginal costs are only ruinous if they consistently fail to produce a revenue that covers overheads. The much more positive and useful approach is to aim at maximising *contribution* to produce bigger profits. This can only have a beneficial effect.

In the last chapter, product B produced a greater contribution to profits and overheads than product A, although using an absorption system its profit appeared lower. The correct action in these circumstances is to push sales of B, using the price mechanism where necessary so long as this does not reduce its contribution below the level of A. Only a marginal costing approach provides this lead.

## 6.5. PARETO'S LAW

Vilfredo Pareto was an Italian economist who originally made the deceptively simple statement that the wealth of any nation is held by a small percentage of its population. The 'law', also known as the '80-20 Rule', has a number of applications in management accounting, so much so that it could have been introduced in almost any chapter.

The law has been refined by accountants and economists to suggest that in many business situations 20 per cent of the causes produce 80 per cent of the effects. For example, it is frequently the case that approximately 20 per cent of all items of cost account for around 80 per cent of the total costs in monetary terms, leading to the conclusion that most of the available time and effort should be spent controlling the cost categories which, although small in number, have a big effect on the total.

In pricing, a small number of products often provide the bulk of the contribution to profit and overheads. So the message is clear: if time is at a premium businesses should concentrate on those few goods and services which are important and leave the large remainder to look after themselves.

## 6.6. CONCLUSION

This subject has been dealt with briefly, reflecting its simplicity rather than its lack of importance.

Increasing prices will normally be the simplest way of improving profits for most smaller businesses: perhaps this is the reason why so many consider it last.

### References
[1] Wood, E.G.: *Bigger Profits for the Smaller Firm*. Business Books, 1972.
[2] Aydon, C. (of Cyril Aydon Associates), unpublished text.

### Further reading
[1] Wood, E.G.: *op. cit.*
[2] British Institute of Management leaflet: *'Pareto's Principle — The 80-20 Rule'*, in the 'Guidelines for the Small Business' series.

CHAPTER 7

# Cost-Volume-Profit Relationships

## 7.1. INTRODUCTION

Cost, revenue, volume and profit are factors which have been mentioned a number of times already, but the relationship which always exists between them in any business situation has not been fully explored. The interaction between sales in monetary and volume terms and costs separated into their fixed and variable elements is one of the most significant features of any business: it holds the key to success. To take decisions without an understanding of how the relationship alters with changing circumstances is to court disaster: it is of prime importance to the lending banker, particularly if money is requested for expansion. Unless he can understand how the cost-volume-profit structure of a business submitting an application will be affected by a proposed investment, a banker may have little idea whether the lending will be in the company's best interests or not. A knowledge of the basic concepts is easy to acquire and enables bankers to assess fully the information supplied by good customers. It also helps us to encourage our poorer ones to produce it.

## 7.2. BREAK-EVEN ANALYSIS

Fortunately, the relationship lends itself to graphical representation in the shape of what are known as break-even charts. These are usually simple to plot and provide a useful and revealing picture of a business: 'The break-even point is important to management . . . since it marks the very lowest level to which activity can drop without putting the continued life of the company in jeopardy'.[1]

Chart 1 shows a typical position in a business over a period of one year. The construction is not difficult:

**a.** Break-even analysis starts with a separation of all costs into those that are fixed and those that are variable. Fixed costs, such as rent and rates, by definition tend to remain unchanged over a period and they can usually be shown as a straight line. In the long run, of course, all costs are variable (new machines are purchased as expansion proceeds) and the relationships shown in a break-even chart can only be valid over a limited time scale.

*Chart 1* **Traditional break-even chart**

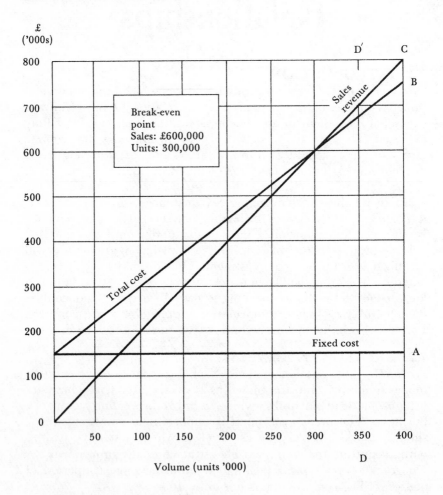

**£ ('000s)**

Break-even point
Sales: £600,000
Units: 300,000

Sales revenue

Total cost

Fixed cost

Volume (units '000)

*Basis*
Selling price = £2
Variable cost = £1.50
Fixed costs = £150,000

In this example, fixed costs are represented by a straight line A drawn at a level of £150,000.

**b.** Variable costs are those that tend to increase in total in proportion to units of output, such as raw materials, and are plotted above the fixed costs to give line B. They are incurred in this company at the rate of £1.50 per unit and can easily be read off in total at any point.

**c.** The sales revenue line C is plotted by multiplying the number of units by the unit selling price, which is £2 in this example.

**d.** The chart has little value unless the various lines are related to an estimated level of activity. In this case the managers of the business have decided that the most likely level of output is 350,000 units, represented by line D-D'. This is also the company's maximum capacity.

It must be made clear that all the figures shown are forecasts; the business is looking ahead, projecting likely levels for costs, volumes and revenues. This will not always be an easy operation and some of the problems are discussed in the next chapter.

Having completed the chart, what is its value?

**a.** It can be seen immediately that the break-even point is reached when the business sells 300,000 units. Below this figure it makes a loss, and above it a profit. The size of the profit or loss for any volume of sales can quickly be read.

**b.** The cost structure of the business can be understood at a glance. The burden of fixed costs is not a slight one but nonetheless it does not look unduly heavy in relation to the variable costs – 21.4 per cent of total sales at full capacity.

**c.** The variable costs appear high. Obviously at any level of activity they absorb 75 per cent of all revenue.

**d.** Break-even is reached very near to the full capacity of the business after over ten months have elapsed (assuming an even flow of orders during the year). The business needs to be only a small amount adrift in its forecasts or suffer a slight reverse in the market place to make a loss. This gap between break-even and full capacity is known as the 'margin of safety' and in the example is 14.3 per cent of total volume: this can be expressed in number of units or days, i.e. 50,000 units or 52 days (14.3 per cent of 365).

**e.** A comparatively large rise in sales is required to provide a relatively small increase in profits. This is better explained by drawing a second chart.

*Chart 2* **Break-even chart with variable costs at base**

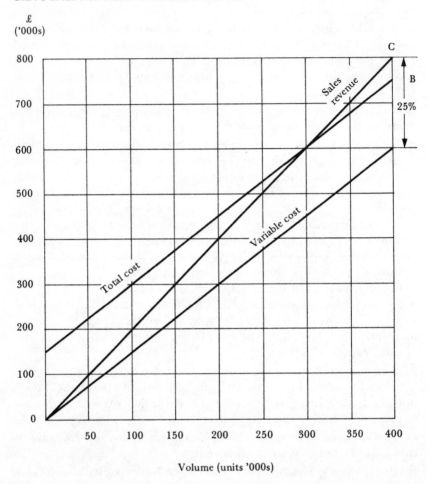

Volume (units '000s)

This chart differs from the first only in layout; the lines for sales revenue and total costs are unchanged. It is a more useful format for several reasons:

**a.** It can be used to illustrate a marginal costing approach. The difference between the variable cost line and the sales revenue total at any point represents the contribution to fixed costs (overheads) and profit.

**b.** Because the chart has been drawn with straight lines the relationship of contribution to sales is constant throughout the year at a figure of 25 per cent. This is called the 'profit-volume ratio' and indicates in this example that, say, a doubling of sales would continue to produce a 25 per cent contribution, assuming that the underlying cost structure of the business remains unaltered (in practice, this is unlikely to happen and the effect of such a change on a break-even chart is examined in a moment).

**c.** Placing fixed costs on top suggests rightly that they are a burden to be borne by the contribution.

**d.** The effect on the break-even point of any change in fixed costs can be readily measured without drawing a new chart.

Overall, this business has little room for error: it breaks even very close to its maximum capacity; has a low margin of safety; and could easily end the year making a loss. It is, however, typical of many thousands of firms.

By way of contrast, Chart 3 shows a much healthier business, although it has to be admitted that it is a picture seen only very infrequently.

This company breaks even after three months, having sold only 25 per cent of the expected total volume for the year. It has a high margin of safety at 75 per cent and can afford to suffer a large drop in sales or a heavy increase in costs before it loses profitability. It also has a high profit-volume ratio – 80 per cent – indicating a large contribution from each unit sold; a small increase in turnover will bring a large increase in profits. Costs are low, particularly its variable costs – direct labour and materials – and the company is able to obtain good margins. This indicates a possible danger in the situation, for unless the company's products are protected in some way (e.g. by patent), such a lucrative market is likely to attract a flood of competitors who will drive prices down.

How can the first business become more like the second? What can be done to improve the relationship between the three important factors in the equation? The charts highlight the main alternatives:

**a.** Raise prices.

**b.** Increase sales volume.

**c.** Reduce costs.

These choices are very important and worth examining individually. It is worth stressing that they are three of only four ways in which any business can increase its profits; the fourth – improving the product mix - will be dealt with briefly at the end of this chapter.

*Chart 3* **Break-even chart: healthy business**

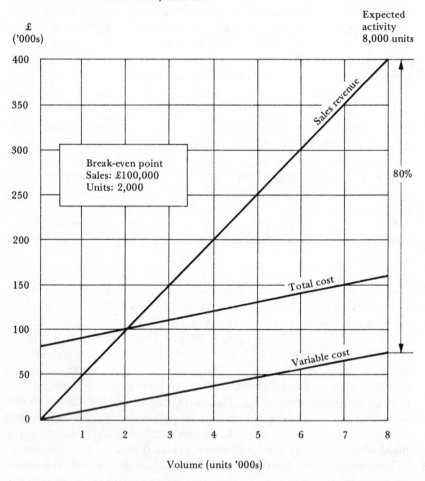

Volume (units '000s)

*Basis*
Selling price = £50
Variable cost = £10
Fixed costs = £80,000

There are no others. If a business is seeking to improve its profits by using a method which does not produce one or more of these results, then its efforts will be wasted.

## a. Raising prices

The broad implications of raising prices were discussed in Chapter 6, but at this stage more specific considerations can be examined. Although increasing prices is frequently the quickest and easiest way of lifting profits, it will sometimes be accompanied by a drop in volume. Incidentally, this is by no means as common as many business managers believe; much depends on the product, the nature of the industry and the general state of the market. In times of high inflation people become accustomed to price rises, with the result that their spending pattern changes little unless their purchasing power is reduced or they are confronted with increases in certain areas which appear unreasonable. Even in times of economic depression, increasing prices can be the best policy, as with the well-known case of the perfume manufacturer in the United States that raised its selling prices during the Second World War at a time when all other producers were frantically dropping theirs in an attempt to stimulate demand. Far from decreasing its volume, the company saw the reverse effect as homecoming soldiers rushed to buy their wives and sweethearts the most expensive perfume available.

For the sake of illustration, in this example it will be assumed that an increase of 10 per cent in selling prices will cause a drop in demand of 5 per cent. This means that at a full capacity of 350,000 units (see Chart 2) the revenue will increase to £731,500 (332,500 x £2.20). Where there is uncertainty about the exact reaction of the market, it is a simple procedure to produce a chart showing revenues over a range of price increases and volumes.

## b. Increasing sales volume

The main question for businesses under this heading is, 'how much extra turnover is required to double or treble profit?' We have already seen that this is closely linked to the relative proportions of variable and fixed costs: a small increase in sales can sometimes produce a large increase in profits. The key indicator is the profit-volume ratio.

## c. Reducing costs

This is an important area and one that could justify a chapter to itself. As a means of increasing profitability it is the most difficult heading under which to achieve worthwhile results and the most demanding of managerial time and effort. Nevertheless it can produce valuable results, and in times like the present it may be the only possible way for a business to survive when prices are controlled and economic conditions render it impossible to achieve an increase in sales.

A cost reduction programme should never be entered into lightly. It is hard work and causes more internal resistance than any other method. There are three cardinal rules:

*i* Concentrate on significant costs – this is a further application of Pareto's Law: all effort should be concentrated on those items which, although small in number, comprise a large percentage of total costs in terms of value. Because they are so significant, small reductions of 1 or 2 per cent will often mean large overall savings. This is contrary to what happens in many businesses, where a manager who spends most of his time racing around the office telling typists to use carbons until they disintegrate and make all their telephone calls after 1 o'clock may feel he has achieved a great deal, but at the end of the day the net result will probably only be an increase in his blood pressure coupled with a negligible saving in costs. The real offence is that his efforts will probably distract his attention from the expenses that are significant. Also, the tiny savings he has produced will almost certainly be short-lived when other pressures force him away from a close supervision of his typists. This syndrome has been well recognised by Peter Drucker: 'The annual cost-reduction drive . . . is as predictable in most businesses as a head cold in spring. It is about as enjoyable. But six months later costs are back where they were'.[2]

*ii* Concentrate on costs that are easy to reduce – which items are not essential to the survival of the business? What can a company stop spending money on or delay purchasing without endangering its existence? It is difficult to lay down hard and fast rules because much will depend on individual circumstances, but examples might be advertising, consultancy or redecorating. This is complementary to reducing significant costs, not a substitute. Items which are important must not be ignored simply because they are difficult to reduce.

*iii* Work to a plan – the need for proper planning is no less important in a cost reduction programme than it is in any other area of management accounting. An organised approach is likely to be much more effective than a series of spasmodic outbursts.

Suppose the company seeking improvement has managed to gain

a 10 per cent reduction in both fixed and variable costs; the complete effect on its position can quickly be seen from a new break-even chart.

*Chart 4* **Revised version of Chart 2**

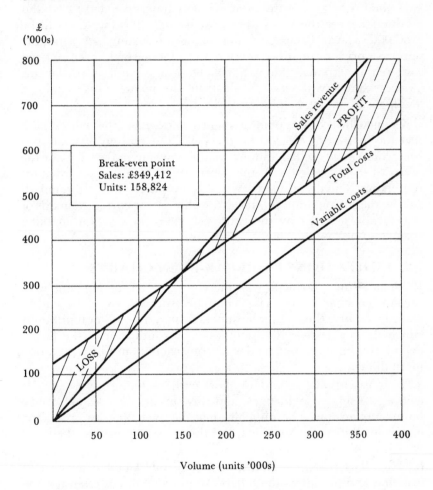

£
('000s)

Break-even point
Sales: £349,412
Units: 158,824

Sales revenue

PROFIT

Total costs

Variable costs

LOSS

Volume (units '000s)

*Basis*
Selling price = £2.20
Variable cost = £1.35
Fixed costs = £135,000

The business is much healthier. The break-even point occurs earlier in the year, with a corresponding increase in the margin of safety. The profit-volume ratio has also improved.

At this point the company managers wonder whether an investment in new capital equipment part way through the year is feasible. Their longer-term objective is growth, and they feel that this might be a good time to buy the necessary machinery needed to expand production over the years. The cost during the first year will be £150,000 (as was discussed in the chapter on costing, this is not the purchase price of the machinery but the increased burden of fixed costs required to maintain it. Such a large sum is unrealistic for this business but it will serve to illustrate the point). Once again, a break-even chart is helpful (see Chart 5).

The new break-even point is slightly in excess of the revised sales revenue figure of £731,500 for the year. The margin of safety has been completely eroded and the company would make a loss for the period if it proceeded with the expenditure. The position requires rethinking. The investment might still be worthwhile if the imbalance in the cost-volume-profit relationship can be corrected in this or later years, perhaps by the extra volume of production enabling savings to be made in the variable costs.

## 7.3. LIMITATIONS OF BREAK-EVEN CHARTS

If business management was merely a matter of juggling with break-even charts, achieving company success would be child's play. In reality, the technique suffers from a number of limitations which do not destroy its usefulness as an indicator of the future health of a business but render its construction and interpretation more difficult:

**a.** It is essentially an aid to short-term planning. The chart is compiled using straight lines, and this can only hold good over a limited time-span. The difficulty may be overcome by producing curves for the factors involved, but this presupposes that the basic data is available.

**b.** The chart presumes that a change in one factor can occur in isolation and not affect the others. In practice this is often not the case.

**c.** It presumes that the product mix remains static. This is unhelpful, particularly if a change in the mix is being considered as a means of improving profitability; for example, a marginal costing approach might have pinpointed those products providing a high contribution and the business may quite properly wish to concentrate its resources on their manufacture and sale. The alternative is to produce different charts for each possible mix and this is perfectly

*Chart 5* **Inclusion of capital investment**

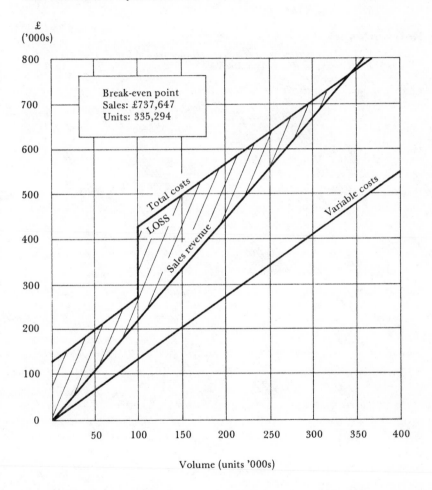

Volume (units '000s)

*Basis*
Selling price = £2.20
Variable cost = £1.35
Fixed costs = £285,000

feasible. The services of a computer can be utilised if the range is wide.

**d.** The chart takes no account of stock changes. This is not really a disadvantage so far as decision-making is concerned, but it is a point to be borne in mind when comparing the results with those portrayed in the audited accounts.

## References

[1] Harper, W.M.: *Management Accounting.* 2nd ed. Macdonald and Evans, 1977.
[2] Drucker, P.: *Managing for Results.* Pan, 1967.

CHAPTER 8

# Planning for Profit
# I - Budgets

## 8.1. THE IMPORTANCE OF BUDGETING

Many businesses fail to make a reasonable profit or to generate sufficient cash at the right time because management fails to plan ahead. As bankers are only too aware, the profit or loss is often not known until many months after the end of the financial year, and a cash shortage is only seen when a crisis point is reached.

The uncomfortable predicament of a banker being asked to reach a decision on a request for an increased facility and being faced with a set of accounts many months out of date is disturbingly familiar. Budgeting can provide much assistance in these circumstances, since it requires business management to look ahead and forces it to stand back from the situation where it is continually and exclusively solving yesterday's problems.

Every business, no matter how small, needs a budget. To be without one is like a ship without a course, cruising along blissfully unaware of how far off the best route it is or which rocks it is likely to hit next; only sheer luck can save it from misfortune and misadventure.

## 8.2. WHAT IS A BUDGET?

Put simply, a budget is management's plans for a business expressed in financial terms. It may be the size of an envelope or it may run to many volumes. It should be based on predetermined objectives. It should represent what is most likely to happen after a careful balance has been struck between the ambitions of management and the constraints on the business. There are three main types of budget of interest to bankers:

**a. Operating budgets** – these set out the plans for the trading operations. They will normally show the profit or loss at the end of a period and are not concerned with cash, although, as we shall see later, they are a necessary preliminary to a cash flow forecast.

**b. Capital budgets** – lists of proposed expenditures on capital projects. They are required for inclusion in cash flow forecasts but not operating budgets. Before any item appears in this budget, it should have undergone a sound procedure of appraisal. The main methods of appraisal in common use are covered in the next chapter.

**c. Cash budgets** – alternatively termed cash flow forecasts or cash plans. These will be discussed in Chapter 10.

## 8.3. OBJECTIVES OF BUDGETS

Soundly completed and properly monitored, a budget will be of assistance in three major ways:

**a. In providing a plan** – showing where the business is intended to go, when action is required and what the results of this action are likely to be. It enables management to sit down and plot its profitability and liquidity for a future period. How often do bankers see customers anticipating profits that never materialise or spending money because their banking accounts are in credit, only to find that their excessive liquidity is short-lived? The only solution is a map showing the desired path for a business.

**b. In aiding control** – by the comparison of actual figures against the budget. This is a key part of the budgeting process. Actual results must be compared at regular intervals with those expected and corrective action taken as appropriate. This is an integral step; to ignore it is to lose much of the benefit of the technique. There is little point in the captain of a ship failing to check his actual position against his planned course, and the same is true of the manager of a business. This system of comparison is known as *budgetary control*.

**c. In helping to co-ordinate the operations of a business** – by identifying the responsibilities of managers at various levels. As a business grows, it becomes increasingly difficult for the senior executives to control its activities and they are forced to delegate. This can be just as difficult, particularly where the people who own and manage the business are one and the same and have built it up from nothing over a number of years, but their ability to delegate without loss of control will indicate their success as managers and will be directly responsible for the fortunes or otherwise of the business as it expands. Budgeting is an important aid to delegation, because managers lower down the scale can be set targets which have a place in the overall plan; control being maintained by regular monitoring and the reporting of variances. The human aspects of budgeting cannot be ignored and it is important to involve all managers in the setting of targets. This not only ensures that the operations of the company are properly co-ordinated, but also helps to motivate the people concerned.

None of these objectives will be met unless the system of budgeting has the full support of senior management. The plan is for everyone in the company and it starts at the top.

## 8.4. PREPARING A BUDGET

The remainder of this chapter discusses the preparation and interpretation of operating budgets, with comments being built around the forecasts of the managers of *XL Engineering*.

Figure 1 shows their first-ever attempt at budgeting. It covers a complete financial year from 1 July 1978 to 30 June 1979. Ideally this budget should have been completed several weeks before the start of the period, but in this case the directors were not aware of the technique until September 1978 so the first two months show actual figures and the remainder are projections.

How have the figures been produced?

**a.** It is important to stress at the outset that the amounts shown should represent the carefully considered views of the management of the business. They should express the best estimates of what is most likely to happen, using all the forecasting skills the managers possess or can acquire.

**b.** The figures should be as realistic as possible: allowances should be made for all expected price changes for both inputs and outputs, whether caused by inflation or otherwise; consideration should be given to the prevailing economic conditions and the general state of the industry; and account should be taken of any limiting factors which may constrain the ambitions of the company, e.g. lack of productive capacity, shortage of key personnel, delays in the delivery of raw materials, inadequate storage space, and inadequate working capital.

**c.** Sales is the vital figure. Most of the other amounts are linked to it, either directly or indirectly, and a poor sales forecast will cause repercussions throughout the budget. It is usually the most difficult item to complete and is the greatest stumbling block to the introduction of budgeting, because many managers feel that it is impossible to forecast future demand in their industry. In all but a few businesses this is a convenient excuse for inactivity. In practice, there are

*Figure 1*

## XL Engineering operating budget for twelve months ending 30.6.79

(All figures in '000s)

|  | July | Aug | Sept | Oct | Nov | Dec | Jan | Feb | Mar | Apr | May | June | Total |
|---|---|---|---|---|---|---|---|---|---|---|---|---|---|
| Sales – home | 17 | 17 | 18 | 18 | 21 | 21 | 21 | 21 | 23 | 23 | 25 | 25 | 250 |
| export | 53 | 53 | 57 | 57 | 64 | 64 | 64 | 64 | 67 | 67 | 70 | 70 | 750 |
| Total sales | 70 | 70 | 75 | 75 | 85 | 85 | 85 | 85 | 90 | 90 | 95 | 95 | 1,000 |
| Direct material purchases | 40 | 40 | 35 | 35 | 90 | 90 | 90 | 90 | 45 | 45 | 50 | 50 | 700 |
| Direct labour | 5 | 5 | 5 | 5 | 5 | 5 | 5 | 5 | 5 | 5 | 5 | 5 | 60 |
| Stock change (increase)/decrease | — | — | 25 | 25 | (50) | (50) | (50) | (50) | 25 | 25 | 25 | 25 | (50) |
| Cost of goods sold | 45 | 45 | 65 | 65 | 45 | 45 | 45 | 45 | 75 | 75 | 80 | 80 | 710 |
| Gross profit | 25 | 25 | 10 | 10 | 40 | 40 | 40 | 40 | 15 | 15 | 15 | 15 | 290 |
| Overheads |  |  |  |  |  |  |  |  |  |  |  |  |  |
| Production costs | 2 | 2 | 1 | 1 | 10 | 10 | 10 | 10 | 3 | 3 | 4 | 4 | 60 |
| Selling & distribution costs | 5 | 5 | 5 | 5 | 6 | 6 | 6 | 6 | 8 | 8 | 10 | 10 | 80 |
| Administrative costs | 7 | 8 | 8 | 9 | 9 | 9 | 10 | 10 | 10 | 10 | 10 | 10 | 110 |
| Other expenses | — | 1 | — | 1 | 5 | 10 | 5 | 3 | 1 | 1 | 1 | 3 | 30 |
| Depreciation | — | — | 1 | 1 | 1 | 1 | 1 | 1 | 1 | 1 | 1 | 1 | 10 |
| Net profit before tax | 11 | 9 | (5) | (7) | 9 | 4 | 8 | 10 | (8) | (7) | (11) | (13) | Nil |

*Supporting schedules would show full details where appropriate.*

a number of useful aids to sales forecasting which will often provide estimates of sufficient accuracy, particularly after managers have become experienced in their use:

*i* Past trends - obviously the first aspect to consider is how the business has fared in the past. This will expose many unrealistic projections straightaway; far too many businesses begin by suggesting a level of turnover that bears no relation to anything that has been achieved previously. The sophistication of this part of the exercise depends on the size and nature of the business; some will certainly wish to break down their sales total into product ranges or groups of services.

*ii* Reports from salesmen – these are the people in the business who should have the best feel for what is happening to consumer demand at grass roots level. They are in constant touch with customers. It is my experience, however, that salesmen rarely take an unjaundiced view, being optimists by nature.

*iii* Market analysis – there are a number of organisations in many countries equipped to conduct detailed surveys into most markets at home and abroad, often producing excellent results. This tends to be an expensive service and is probably not one for the small business unless it is contemplating devoting a large percentage of its resources to a new or redesigned product.

*iv* Order books – this is the simplest way to calculate a part of the sales for a forthcoming period.

*v* Tenders – an examination of tenders submitted over the past few months, allied to the company's usual success rate, provides a good indication of likely future orders.

*vi* Contact customers – a number of customers will have completed their own budgets in which they will have made allowance for their purchases. They will not normally object to providing an indication of their plans. Some businesses are reluctant to ask for this information but they should remember that a supplier's continued existence can be of great importance to many of their customers.

*vii* General business trends – what is happening to the market? Is technological innovation rendering some products obsolete? Are cheaper products from overseas proving stiff competition? Is the industry expanding or declining?

*viii* Seasonality – there is little point in a manufacturer of Christmas tree decorations budgeting for an even level of sales throughout the year.

*ix* Exports – these should be considered separately, as timings are often more difficult to forecast.

*x* The executive panel method – this can sometimes work extremely well. It involves pooling management opinion from all levels and areas of the business, using either formal methods such as committees and reports or simply informal discussions.

**d.** The sales figures lead directly to the company's requirement for raw materials. The question to be answered is 'what materials are we required to purchase to match the levels of production needed to meet our sales targets and at what cost, bearing in mind increases or decreases in stock levels?' The management's policy regarding stock holding is of great importance. This will be discussed in Chapter 12.

**e.** Next the business must decide what labour it needs to achieve the desired level of production and at what cost. In practice, this cost is rarely as variable as management accountants would like to pretend.

**f.** The forecast for other direct costs and overheads is normally the easiest part of the budget to complete because it will be largely composed of those costs that tend to be fixed, such as office salaries, and those that tend to vary in proportion to the estimated level of sales or production such as power. The main concern is to ensure that all expenses affecting the net profit are included; the most commonly encountered items inadvertently omitted are depreciation and finance charges. It is sometimes worth including a notional rent charge for freehold properties, as this brings to the businessman's attention the reality that he is using in his business a scarce resource which is costing money, in the sense that the opportunity exists to sell the asset and invest the proceeds. (This is a good example of one of the strengths of management accounting; it is not constrained by any principles of financial accounting, and the information can be produced in a form which is most useful to those who manage the business.)

As this is an operating budget, any cash movements which are not charges or additions to the profit figure will be excluded, e.g. capital expenditure.

**g.** In all businesses, except those that are wholly or partially 'exempt', value added tax should not be added to the budget figures, since such amounts are either payable to, or recoverable from Customs and Excise and their inclusion would distort the budgeted profit.

It must, however, be included in cash flow forecasts, where its incidence can have far-reaching implications.

Before turning to an interpretation of the figures produced by *XL Engineering*, it is worth re-emphasising two points. First, an operating budget has nothing necessarily to do with *cash*, the budgeted amounts being those which are expected to appear in the *books of the company* for a particular period; thus, a projected sale is shown during the month when the goods leave the factory or an invoice is raised. Secondly, the preparation of a budget is not merely an accounting function; it is the responsibility of top management, who must give it their full support. In almost every case where budgeting and budgetary control fail, it is through the lack of involvement and support from the senior executives of the company.

The picture for *XL Engineering* looks bleak. The good profits it has earned in previous years are forecast to disappear. A small variance in the actual figures will cause the business to make a loss and, in any case, some of the costs for the year are being carried forward in the increased holding of stock.

Herein lies the immense value of budgeting. The XL managers are able to take decisions about the future path of the business with adequate time at their disposal; they are not forced into panic action when the true position is suddenly revealed in their audited accounts many months after the end of the 1979 financial year.

What action can they take? Depending on the circumstances, their range of alternatives may be very wide. The most drastic step they could take is to close down the business. Such a move would not be made lightly but it might be the right and proper choice for all interested parties connected with the company if there is no hope of a recovery in the longer term. Far too few businesses assess the future viability of their operations at regular intervals, with the consequence that many continue trading far past the point where shareholders and outside creditors could be paid a realistic dividend in a liquidation. However unpalatable the decision, delays will not aid a business with a fundamental and irreversible imbalance in its cost-volume-profit structure. Budgets are the only tools which can give managers the information they need for this decision.

Fortunately, other realistic options are available to the senior managers of *XL Engineering*. After a thorough examination of all possible avenues and in consultation with managers from all levels, they are confident they can avert a crisis by increasing prices overseas by 10 per cent and reducing administrative overheads by 20 per cent. Figure 2 shows the redrawn budget. The company feels that a

*Figure 2*

## XL Engineering revised operating budget for twelve months ending 30.6.79

(All figures in '000s)

|  | July | Aug | Sept | Oct | Nov | Dec | Jan | Feb | Mar | Apr | May | Jun | Total |
|---|---|---|---|---|---|---|---|---|---|---|---|---|---|
| Sales – home | 17 | 17 | 18 | 18 | 21 | 21 | 21 | 21 | 23 | 23 | 25 | 25 | 250 |
| export | 58 | 58 | 63 | 63 | 70 | 70 | 70 | 70 | 74 | 74 | 77 | 78 | 825 |
| Total sales | 75 | 75 | 81 | 81 | 91 | 91 | 91 | 91 | 97 | 97 | 102 | 102 | 1,075 |
| Direct material purchases | 40 | 40 | 35 | 35 | 90 | 90 | 90 | 90 | 45 | 45 | 50 | 50 | 700 |
| Direct labour | 5 | 5 | 5 | 5 | 5 | 5 | 5 | 5 | 5 | 5 | 5 | 5 | 60 |
| Stock change (increase)/decrease | — | — | 25 | 25 | (50) | (50) | (50) | (50) | 25 | 25 | 25 | 25 | (50) |
| Cost of goods sold | 45 | 45 | 65 | 65 | 45 | 45 | 45 | 45 | 75 | 75 | 80 | 80 | 710 |
| Gross profit | 30 | 30 | 16 | 16 | 46 | 46 | 46 | 46 | 22 | 22 | 22 | 23 | 365 |
| Overheads | | | | | | | | | | | | | |
| Production costs | 2 | 2 | 1 | 1 | 10 | 10 | 10 | 10 | 3 | 3 | 4 | 4 | 60 |
| Selling & distribution costs | 5 | 5 | 5 | 5 | 6 | 6 | 6 | 6 | 8 | 8 | 10 | 10 | 80 |
| Administrative costs | 6 | 6 | 6 | 7 | 7 | 8 | 8 | 8 | 8 | 8 | 8 | 8 | 88 |
| Other expenses | — | 1 | — | 1 | 5 | 10 | 5 | 3 | 1 | — | 1 | 3 | 30 |
| Depreciation | — | — | 1 | 1 | 1 | 1 | 1 | 1 | 1 | 1 | 1 | 1 | 10 |
| Net profit before tax | 17 | 16 | 3 | 1 | 17 | 11 | 16 | 18 | 1 | 2 | (2) | (3) | 97 |

*Supporting schedules would show full details where appropriate.*

profit of £97,000 is satisfactory in the light of the economic situation. However, this is by no means the end of the budgetary process.

In order to achieve the targets they have set themselves, the managers will need to ensure that any deviation from their forecast is quickly spotted and the necessary remedial action taken promptly. They will do this by means of a monthly report (Figure 3).

*Figure 3*

**XL Engineering budget report: December 1978**

(All figures in '000s)

|  | This month | | | Year to date | | |
|---|---|---|---|---|---|---|
|  | Budget | Actual | Variance | Budget | Actual | Variance |
| Sales – home | 21 | 21 | — | 112 | 114 | 2 |
| export | 70 | 67 | (3) | 382 | 366 | (16) |
| Total sales | 91 | 88 | (3) | 494 | 480 | (14) |
| Direct material purchases | 90 | 91 | (1) | 330 | 340 | (10) |
| Direct labour | 5 | 5 | — | 30 | 30 | — |
| Stock change (increase)/ decrease | (50) | (48) | (2) | (50) | (50) | — |
| Cost of goods sold | 45 | 48 | (3) | 310 | 320 | (10) |
| Gross profit | 46 | 40 | (6) | 184 | 160 | (24) |
| Overheads | | | | | | |
| Production costs | 10 | 11 | (1) | 26 | 24 | 2 |
| Selling & distribution costs | 6 | 7 | (1) | 32 | 32 | — |
| Administrative costs | 8 | 8 | — | 40 | 40 | — |
| Other expenses | 10 | 9 | 1 | 17 | 19 | (2) |
| Depreciation | 1 | 1 | — | 4 | 4 | — |
| Net profit before tax | 11 | 4 | (7) | 65 | 41 | (24) |

This report clearly shows that the company's operations are not proceeding entirely to plan. It gives the actual figures for December showing an adverse variance of £7,000 in net profit, caused mainly by a higher cost-of-goods-sold figure and smaller shipments abroad than were expected. The cumulative figures from 1 July indicate that this is not an isolated position; the business is running £24,000 short of its profit target. It is obviously having difficulty in keeping down its raw material costs and maintaining its volume of exports.

The examination of these variances is of prime importance. Initially the managers need to discover the cause of the differences. For example, the additional amount of £10,000 spent on direct materials may have arisen for a variety of reasons; price increases, greater usage, higher production levels (the report informs us that this has not, in fact, been the case), changes in the production mix, or any combination. No corrective action is possible until the real cause has been identified. This is the way budgets are used for control; the variances telling managers how far off course they are and indicating whether the problem is in the engine room or another part of the ship. They do not avoid the rocks by themselves – they rely on someone at the wheel understanding the signals and instigating the appropriate avoidance procedure.

## 8.5.  THE VALUE OF BUDGETS TO BANKERS

An operating budget plans and controls the profitability of a business. Management has a tool for pinpointing problem areas almost as quickly as they arise. Corrective action can be initiated promptly, and from the beginning a business may be able to decide on an eventual change of course before it leaves a safe harbour.

I believe these are compelling reasons for bankers asking to see budgets and encouraging their production. They will hardly ever work out exactly in practice, but this is not the point of the exercise – a ship's captain is not sacked because his vessel is 50 miles off course five days out of port; he only courts dismissal if he fails to alter his route. The importance of analysing variances cannot be overstressed; any budget that is left lying in a drawer for 12 months, to be examined only when the lending is due for review, is being grossly misused.

Budgets are as good as the figures they contain. Business customers should be questioned closely on their forecasts and the basic assumptions which have been used in their preparation. There are many reasons why they will not agree with the audited figures, some of which have been discussed. This does not destroy their value; indeed, in view of the many important shortcomings of financial accounting, it probably enhances their usefulness.

Lending bankers should beware of frequent changes in budgets. There is no point in a company continuing to use a budget which has been rendered completely out of date by changing conditions but, on the other hand, it is tempting to some businesses to change their plans to fit their actual results rather than *vice versa*.

Budgetary control is not without its shortcomings. It is a short-term technique which must not be used as a substitute for properly reasoned corporate objectives or strategic planning. In a large company it may be difficult and costly to administer in times of rapid change, although this should be viewed as a reason for streamlining the budgeting process, not abolishing it.

There is no better conclusion to this section than the following extract from an article in *The Banker* by Geoff Wood, Director of Sheffield Polytechnic's Centre for Innovation and Productivity:

'The bank manager can help the owner-manager by showing him how to develop a simple budget. Many managers think that budgeting is a waste of time because it is impossible to forecast future demand in their business. But the purpose of planning is not to see how clever you are at crystal-ball gazing; it is to enable you to make better decisions than you would have made without a plan.

. . . bank managers must warn managers . . . that budgetary control cannot really control a business if it simply consists of looking at last month's figures. It demands that the manager should look ahead to make the kind of decisions that will bring the plans to fruition. First plan your work, then work your plan.'[1]

## Reference

[1] Wood, E.G.: 'The Branch Manager, Small Firm's Friend'. *The Banker*, August 1974.

### Further reading

Powell, R.W.: *Budgetary Control as an Instrument of Management in the Smaller Company*. Industrial and Commercial Finance Corporation, 1971.

CHAPTER 9

# Planning for Profit
# II – Appraising Capital
# Expenditure

## 9.1. FORMIDABLE DECISIONS

Some of the most formidable decisions facing company managers are concerned with the investment of capital in longer-term assets. At the best of times the choice is rarely a straightforward one. During periods like the present it may appear to verge on the impossible. But an attempt must be made to resolve the difficulties, since a decision to invest a significant sum in fixed assets usually shapes the structure of a business for many years, and a reversal of policy will often involve the sale of assets at a loss as well as leaving the enterprise in a considerably weakened position. Any business can quickly be faced with serious problems if a capital purchase has been made solely on the basis of short-lived opportunities or without proper appraisal.

The subject is of vital relevance to bankers, not solely because we lend money over the medium term to finance this type of expenditure, but also for the reason that a bad investment decision can lead to a fundamental imbalance arising in the cost-volume-profit relationship, e.g. an increased level of overheads causing a reduction in the margin of safety (see Chapter 7). Once again, this emphasises the need to look ahead, to produce a proper plan for the effects any major expenditures will have on the profitability and liquidity of the business. All too frequently this is not done; a businessman sees a credit balance on his current account and rushes to buy a new piece of machinery which took his fancy at a recent trade fair, without pausing to consider the drain on his working capital position over the life of the asset or the overall impact on profitability.

The managers of a business should always ask themselves why the investment is being made – this is another area where there is no substitute for clear objectives. The answer should be to recoup more money over a period of time than has been spent on the capital item, bearing in mind the other cash needs of the business and any alternative investments which may be available. Many businessmen will say they invest because of 'need'. This position often makes some sense – a company manufacturing plastic products which has suffered an irreparable breakdown in its only injection moulding machine must obviously purchase a new one in order to continue its activities – but there should still be some other type of appraisal. The higher annual running costs of the new machine might mean that the business cannot earn an adequate return without taking one of the four steps to improve profits discussed in a previous chapter. And what happens if none of these is practicable? The business is in a much more serious position than it would have been with only a broken machine. Many companies take the decision to move to bigger and better premises simply because they are cramped in their existing ones – if only business life could be that uncomplicated!

These points serve to emphasise three important aspects of capital investment appraisal. First, it is concerned with choosing from alternatives; a business always has a choice. It may be as complex as deciding, faced with a large number of possible sites, where to locate several overseas subsidiaries, or as uncluttered as judging whether or not a single item of equipment should be purchased. Secondly, all measurements are made in cash flow terms. The test is whether cash inflows exceed cash outflows by a sufficient margin to be acceptable to the managers of a business, regardless of their usual treatment for accounting purposes. Thus the traditional distinction between 'capital' and 'revenue' has no place in appraisal techniques. Thirdly, any method should ideally enable comparisons to be made between the earnings from the project and the cost to the business of the funds used to finance it.

## 9.2. WHAT IS CAPITAL EXPENDITURE?

When asked this question most bankers immediately think of those assets which go 'below the line', such as a new or extended factory or an investment in additional plant and machinery. But a broader definition than this is preferable. S.V. Bishop[1] has recommended a useful range of characteristics:
– They are not absolutely essential for the immediate day-to-day operations.
– They bring about major changes in the future.
– They are once-off, infrequent and non-routine.
– They cut across traditional lines of organisation and require closer than normal working relationships between junior managers of different functions.

In addition to the examples already mentioned other items which would be included are: the introduction of a new product or the complete redesign of an existing line; employing significant numbers of additional staff to cope with a new contract or the development of a nationwide servicing facility; a 'lease or buy' decision; major promotions, sponsorships or advertising campaigns; or the installation of expensive new accounting machinery.

## 9.3. METHODS OF APPRAISAL
There are four main methods of appraisal. They have in common a concern with cash flows. They all therefore require an evaluation of: the initial cost, the running expenses, the estimated life of the project, and the income over the life of the project. Only cash items are included in the calculation of these factors. This means that depreciation is ignored, but the expected residual value of the item in the market place is included. Or, put another way; the book entries for depreciation need not be made since the effects of depreciation are reflected in the anticipated sales proceeds which are included amongst the cash inflows. Taxation, which may be a cash inflow or outflow, can have a significant effect on an investment decision and should always be included.

The four methods are payback, average rate of return, net present value, and yield or internal rate of return.

### a. Payback
This method calculates the time required for cash inflows to recoup the initial investment on the project. The payback period indicates to management the time that the investment is at risk; the shorter the length of the period to payback the better.

Consider a company which is replacing a machine and is faced with three alternatives, all of which meet the necessary technical specifications.

Machine B covers its cost in the shortest time, just 2 years 8 months after purchase. Machines A and C take considerably longer and on the face of it there is little to choose between them, although C is more expensive to purchase. Any management considering this method of appraisal only would have no hesitation in deciding to buy machine B.

This method is widely used because it is simple to understand. It should not be underrated since it provides a clear indication of the time required to convert a risky investment (and no investments are free of risk) into a safe one.

(All figures in '000s)

| | Machine A £ | Machine B £ | Machine C £ |
|---|---|---|---|
| Cash price and all other initial costs | 50.0 | 50.0 | 70.0 |
| Net cash inflows Year | | | |
| 1 | 5.0 | 15.0 | 10.0 |
| 2 | 10.0 | 25.0 | 10.0 |
| 3 | 15.0 | 15.0 | 20.0 |
| 4 | 20.0 | 5.0 | 20.0 |
| 5 | 20.0 | 5.0 | 30.0 |
| 6 | 15.0 | – | 20.0 |
| 7 | – | – | 10.0 |
| Residual value (at end of last operating year) | 1.0 | – | 2.0 |
| | 86.0 | 65.0 | 122.0 |
| Payback | 4 years | 2²⁄₃ years | 4⅓ years |

In times like the present this can be an overriding consideration, particularly when there are large differences between the various options available. It does not, however, pay any heed to several important factors: the timing of cash flows; the situation after the payback period; and the return on capital invested.

**b.  Average rate of return**
This method calculates the average annual net cash inflow as a percentage of the initial cash outflow. This may be represented by the formula:

$$\frac{\text{Average annual net cash inflow}}{\text{Initial cash outlay}}$$

For the example used to illustrate the first method the calculations are:

(All figures in '000s)

| | Machine A | Machine B | Machine C |
|---|---|---|---|
| Period generated | 6 years | 5 years | 7 years |
| | £ | £ | £ |
| Total net cash inflows | 86.0 | 65.0 | 122.0 |
| Average annual cash inflows | 14.333 | 13.0 | 17.429 |
| Initial cash outlay | 50.0 | 50.0 | 70.0 |
| Average rate of return | 28.7% | 26% | 24.9% |

This provides an entirely different kind of yardstick, which indicates the return earned on the capital employed. Although there is no large disparity between the figures, machine A has displaced B as the best choice with machine C remaining in third place.

This method also has the advantage of simplicity, but continues to ignore the timing of cash flows.

## c. Net present value

Money can be said to have a time value. £1 today is worth more than £1 in a year's time because it can be invested to earn interest. How much more it is worth will depend upon the rate of interest it can earn during the year. If it can be used to buy stocks or bonds paying 10 per cent per annum, then it will be worth £1.10 in one year's time. Expressed another way, £1 received in one year's time is equivalent to 91p today (91p + 10% = £1). Incidentally this concept does not rely on the effects of inflation. It applies equally well to periods with a nil rate of inflation. High rates of inflation merely increase the discount factors, since interest rates will generally be pitched at a higher level.

The two methods discussed so far have failed to recognise this concept and this is an important limitation. To arrive at a proper appraisal an allowance must be made for the timing of cash flows, and this is done by reducing the value of future incomings and outgoings to their present-day worth, using an appropriate rate of interest. This process is known as *discounting* and the factors may be calculated using the formula:

$$\frac{1}{(1 + i)^n}$$

where 'i' is the rate of interest and 'n' the number of years. In practice, it is much easier to look up the figures in the tables; these are provided in Appendix 1.

This method is most easily explained by looking at the example which assesses the same three machines examined above.

This provides a clear indication of the value of the cash flows after due allowance has been given for the year in which they are received. A 10 per cent discount rate has been assumed; the factor chosen should normally represent the required earnings rate of the business. If the rate is chosen in this way, then the appraisal shows that the project is desirable so long as the total present value of the net cash inflows exceeds the initial outlay. In this example all three invest-

| | 10% Discount | Machine A Actual value | Present value | Machine B Actual value | Present value | Machine C Actual value | Present value |
|---|---|---|---|---|---|---|---|
| | £ | £ | | £ | | £ | |
| Initial cash outflow | 1 | 50,000 | 50,000 | 50,000 | 50,000 | 70,000 | 70,000 |
| Net cash inflows Year | | | | | | | |
| 1 | .909 | 5,000 | 4,545 | 15,000 | 13,635 | 10,000 | 9,090 |
| 2 | .826 | 10,000 | 8,260 | 25,000 | 20,650 | 10,000 | 8,260 |
| 3 | .751 | 15,000 | 11,265 | 15,000 | 11,265 | 20,000 | 15,020 |
| 4 | .683 | 20,000 | 13,660 | 5,000 | 3,415 | 20,000 | 13,660 |
| 5 | .621 | 20,000 | 12,420 | 5,000 | 3,105 | 30,000 | 18,630 |
| 6 | .564 | 15,000 | 8,460 | – | – | 20,000 | 11,280 |
| 7 | .513 | – | – | – | – | 10,000 | 5,130 |
| Residual value | | 1,000 | 564 | – | – | 2,000 | 1,026 |
| | | 86,000 | 59,174 | 65,000 | 52,070 | 122,000 | 82,096 |

ments meet this criterion (if they did not, then they would be rejected using this method of appraisal):

Machine A – Net present value of inflows exceeds initial outflow by £9,174.

Machine B – Net present value of inflows exceeds initial outflow by £2,070.

Machine C – Net present value of inflows exceeds initial outflow by £12,096.

Since no clear-cut alternative has emerged as the most desirable, there is a need for further analysis. Whilst machine C produces the largest excess, it is the most expensive and it is not immediately clear how it rates alongside machine A. To provide an additional assessment of the merits of each investment, the discounted inflows can be related to the original outlay to complete what is known as the 'profitability index':

| | Machine A | Machine B | Machine C |
|---|---|---|---|
| Profitability index | 59,174 / 50,000 | 52,070 / 50,000 | 82,096 / 70,000 |
| = | 1.18 | 1.04 | 1.17 |

The project with the highest profitability index is to be preferred and machine A is therefore the best, albeit by a small margin.

### d. Yield or internal rate of return

This is a refinement of the last method. It is used when managers wish to know the discount rate which exactly equates cash inflows with the outlay. This is sometimes to be preferred to assuming a rate.

The calculation is more time-consuming as it involves using a trial and error method on at least two rates until the two figures are equal. Using machine A as an illustration:

| Year | Cash Flow | Discounted at 14% Factor | Present value | Discounted at 16% Factor | Present value |
|------|-----------|--------------------------|---------------|--------------------------|---------------|
| 1 | 5,000 | .877 | 4,385 | .862 | 4,310 |
| 2 | 10,000 | .769 | 7,690 | .743 | 7,430 |
| 3 | 15,000 | .675 | 10,125 | .641 | 9,615 |
| 4 | 20,000 | .592 | 11,840 | .552 | 11,040 |
| 5 | 20,000 | .519 | 10,380 | .476 | 9,520 |
| 6 | 15,000 | .456 | 6,840 | .410 | 6,150 |
| Residual value | 1,000 | .456 | 456 | .410 | 410 |
| | 86,000 | | 51,716 | | 48,475 |

The correct rate of return lies somewhere between the two and may be determined by interpolation:

$$14 + \left( \frac{51,716}{51,716 + 48,475} \right) \times 2 \ = 15.03\%$$

This rate can then be compared with, say, the rate of any borrowed money which may be required to finance the project or the company's average cost of capital.[2]

## 9.4. SHORTCOMINGS OF APPRAISAL METHODS

Having completed an example, one shortcoming is immediately obvious: not all methods give the same answer. Machine B looked best using the payback technique, but subsequently had the lowest profitability index. The final choice must be made in the light of all the circumstances; it is a matter for managerial judgement as to whether the security of a short payback period outweighs the disadvantage of lower profitability and, incidentally, an undiscounted average rate of return which is slightly less than those of the other options. It is not the task of management accounting to make the decision. It can only pinpoint the merits and shortcomings inherent in each alternative.

The forecasting of cash flows can also pose serious problems. Because of the longer-term nature of most capital investment it is often extremely difficult to project timings and amounts for cash inflows and outflows, particularly during the later stages of the project. This can easily render any appraisal meaningless. Delays in installation of even comparatively simple machinery can quickly cause large variances from the plan, and escalating costs can rapidly eat up margins. In many cases, some proportion of the net cash inflow is represented by expected cost savings, and these are often much more difficult to realise in practice than they are on paper. The machine which was intended to dispense with the services of ten operatives and increase productivity by 30 per cent often looks much less economical after the first year of operation.

It is vital to take all cash items into account when completing the appraisal. It is easy to forget the cost of any additional working capital the project may require, particularly in the area of work-in-progress. Occasionally, new equipment can provide a reduction in the need for working capital and this should not be overlooked as a cash inflow or lower cash outflow.

Taxation has already been mentioned. It is another item which can cause large discrepancies between the actual results and those forecast, frequently because managers feel it is too complicated and difficult a subject to bother with. But often to ignore it is to nullify the value of the appraisal, since projects which appear undesirable before the effects of taxation have been taken into account can look attractive on a post-tax basis. Certainly capital allowances and tax on the earnings from the project must always be included.

Stemming from these problems is the need to be aware of the human element in investment decisions. It is an area of management accounting where the personal hopes and fears of business managers can have a large distorting effect on the figures unless the underlying assumptions are closely questioned. The empire-builder will work hard to produce calculations which purport to justify the investment under consideration, while the manager who is judged solely on the basis of his return on capital employed may be equally industrious in keeping his investment expenditure to a minimum. Thousands of project appraisals must be sanctioned in this country every year on the strength of cash inflows which in the event never materialise because human ambitions had coloured the original estimates. This is often a sin of omission: the production manager conveniently forgetting the increased cost of spare parts or the marketing director ignoring the high stock levels needed for a new product.

These shortcomings do not banish the appraisal methods discussed to perpetual wanderings in the desert of a textbook, but they do increase the need to integrate all capital expenditure into a company's budgeting process.

## 9.5. THE CAPITAL BUDGET

Many companies that assiduously budget their operations and compare actual results against those planned at frequent intervals ignore the value of this mechanism for capital projects in the belief that the original appraisal was sufficient. This loses an invaluable aid to control: a capital budget can quickly spot investments that are running away with themselves; those that are rapidly costing more than planned, where an extrapolation of the figures would show that the project could never be viable. This is a very difficult situation for top management: it is easy to sit back and say, 'our original appraisal has been proved a nonsense, but having invested £10 million already we cannot afford to stop; let's sit tight and see if conditions change to our advantage'. But often a decision to cancel early in the life of a project is much more sensible. There are numerous examples of this dilemma in real life – the Anglo-French Concorde must be the classic of all time (and, incidentally, a prime case of confused objectives causing poor management of resources) – and the only solution is a system which provides close and continuous control. This is capital budgeting. An examination of the types of documents used by businesses under this heading is more than the space considerations of this book will allow, but a number of examples are given by S.V. Bishop.[3]

As is discussed in the next chapter, the figures from the capital budget can be used directly in the preparation of a cash flow forecast. This provides an important check on liquidity; a project which has been evaluated as highly profitable will be a non-starter if it demands cash resources which are not available to the business.

The capital budget also ensures that a business is viewed in its totality. As well as being individually assessed, a possible new project must be examined in the light of its effect on the cost-volume-profit relationship of the enterprise as a whole. All projects seeking approval at any one time should be looked at both separately and collectively to ensure that scarce resources are being used in the most effective way.

## 9.6. QUESTIONS FOR LENDING BANKERS

Bankers are often faced with a request for a facility which will be used in whole or in part for expenditure of a capital nature. The following simple questions should help to establish whether a customer has completed his homework:

– What is the objective of the investment?
– What methods of appraisal have been used?
– Was allowance made for the time value of money?
– What are the amounts and timings of cash flows in both directions?
– Have all cash items been included?
– How accurate are the forecasts? Few forecasts will be entirely correct, but customers sometimes employ tolerances which can provide a useful indication of the margin of safety.
– How will the company exercise control as the investment proceeds?
– Has the effect on the overall financial structure of the business been examined e.g. increased working capital needs?
– Can the business afford it? Do cash plans indicate that there is sufficient liquidity both for the initial investment and the continuing needs during the life of the investment?

The need to question a customer's calculations and assumptions is of crucial importance. The methods of appraisal are merely techniques for presenting a set of cash flows in different ways, and the real skill is in producing the figures in the first place: 'Calculating the correct cash flow is vitally important – and very difficult. Discounting is easy.'[4]

# References and notes

[1] Bishop, S.V.: *Business Planning and Control*. The Institute of Chartered Accountants in England and Wales, 1966.

[2] Not all the authorities agree on the best method of calculating the average cost of capital, but the basic idea is that the cost of each segment of capital is separately assessed and then weighted by the proportion that any particular portion bears to the whole. For further reading on this specific point I suggest J.M. Samuels, and F.M. Wilkes: *Management of Company Finance*. 2nd ed. Nelson, 1975.

[3] Bishop, S.V.: *op. cit.*

[4] Powell, R.W.: *Appraising Capital Investment Proposals*. Industrial and Commercial Finance Corporation, 1975.

# Further reading

I have dealt with this subject very simply and briefly, particularly so far as the methods of appraisal are concerned. My aim has been to show readers that the area is not nearly as complicated as some textbooks would suggest. I hope that for the average reader my brevity will help rather than hinder. I would not pretend that this chapter provides a full exposition of the subject – far from it – and readers are referred to the many works available for more detailed study. Those new to the area might care to start with the useful short ICFC booklet by R.W. Powell, mentioned above.

CHAPTER 10

# Planning for Liquidity I – Cash Flow Forecasts

## 10.1. INTRODUCTION

Cash flow forecasts require little introduction. Most of us will have used them in connection with an advance at one time or another, although some may have doubts about their value. This chapter looks at their aims, their preparation and use, and their value to lending bankers.

Cash flow forecasts are aimed directly at one of the two key ingredients in company success identified in Chapter 4 – liquidity. In the final analysis there is only one reason why a company is forced into liquidation – a shortage of cash to meet its obligations as they fall due. Any business must preserve liquidity to meet its commitments to employees, creditors and shareholders. A full order book is useless without finance to produce the goods. A warehouse stacked to the rafters with finished products will not pay wages if they cannot be converted into cash. High profits will be valueless if financial resources have been over-stretched to earn them. The ability to forecast and regulate the cash requirements of a business must take a high degree of priority.

The terms 'cash budget', 'cash plan' and 'cash flow forecast' are synonymous.

## 10.2. OBJECTIVES OF CASH PLANNING

A cash flow forecast examines the implications of the operating and capital budgets on the cash resources of a business. It is not concerned with a profit or loss, or any items not involving inflows or outflows of cash. It is a vital part of the planning and control mechanism of a business, enabling management to make the fullest use of what is normally a very scarce asset.

How does a cash plan help? First, by assessing that adequate cash will be available to meet the trading needs of the business. Secondly, by assessing that sufficient cash will be available to meet any capital expenditure plans. Thirdly, by facilitating the utilisation of the cash resource of a business to its fullest extent, enabling interest charges on borrowed money to be kept to a minimum and surplus funds to be invested. Lastly, by identifying an approaching cash shortage and thereby enabling management to raise additional funds of the right type and amount.

## 10.3. PREPARING A CASH FLOW FORECAST

For many businesses the preparation of a cash flow forecast is a fairly simple procedure once they have completed their operating and capital expenditure budgets. The forecast is merely a repetition of these budgets with revenue and expenditure staggered to take account of timing differences and with non-cash items excluded. Some companies, particularly very small ones, may attempt to produce a cash plan without the supporting budgets but, whilst this is not impossible, it should not be encouraged since the risk of error is increased. Like most other forms of management accounting the final result is only as good as the figures which have gone into it.

In Chapter 8 a revised operating budget was compiled for *XL Engineering* and this can be used to indicate the various steps necessary in converting the profit and loss figures to the company's first cash plan. Several additional pieces of information are required.

**a. Sales** – home sales are invoiced during the month of despatch and, on average, 20 per cent are paid during the following month, 50 per cent the month after that and the remainder the month after that. Although the company has attempted to streamline its documentation, exports take longer: on average 30 per cent is received during the second month after invoice, 40 per cent the month after and the last 30 per cent suffer another month's delay. Cash sales are negligible and no discounts are offered.

This enables the following schedule to be completed.

The worksheet translates invoiced sales into cash receipts, using the information mentioned earlier. The sales for the four months prior to the commencement of the company's financial year were required to complete the schedule in full and have been assumed. In practice they would be extracted from the books of the company.

**b. Direct materials** – the company endeavours to keep its suppliers reasonably happy by paying 50 per cent the month following receipt of the goods and 50 per cent the month after that. It would be possible to complete a similar schedule to Figure 1 showing this

*Figure 1*

## XL Engineering cash inflows for twelve months ending 30.6.79

(All figures in '000s)

| Month | Sales invoiced Home: Export: | % Home: 20 | % Home: 50 Export: 30 | % Home: 30 Export: 40 | % Export: 30 | Expected cash receipts |
|---|---|---|---|---|---|---|
| 1978 March | 15 | | | | | |
| | 50 | | | | | |
| April | 16 | 3.0 | | | | |
| | 53 | | | | | |
| May | 16 | 3.2 | 7.5 | | | |
| | 53 | | 15.0 | | | |
| June | 16 | 3.2 | 8.0 | 4.5 | | |
| | 53 | | 15.9 | 20.0 | | |
| July | 17 | 3.2 | 8.0 | 4.8 | | 16.0 |
| | 58 | | 15.9 | 21.2 | 15.0 | 52.1 |
| August | 17 | 3.4 | 8.0 | 4.8 | | 16.2 |
| | 58 | | 15.9 | 21.2 | 15.9 | 53.0 |
| Sept. | 18 | 3.4 | 8.5 | 4.8 | | 16.7 |
| | 63 | | 17.4 | 21.2 | 15.9 | 54.5 |
| October | 18 | 3.6 | 8.5 | 5.1 | | 17.2 |
| | 63 | | 17.4 | 23.2 | 15.9 | 56.5 |
| Nov. | 21 | 3.6 | 9.0 | 5.1 | | 17.7 |
| | 70 | | 18.9 | 23.2 | 17.4 | 59.5 |
| Dec. | 21 | 4.2 | 9.0 | 5.4 | | 18.6 |
| | 70 | | 18.9 | 25.2 | 17.4 | 61.5 |
| 1979 January | 21 | 4.2 | 10.5 | 5.4 | | 20.1 |
| | 70 | | 21.0 | 25.2 | 18.9 | 65.1 |
| February | 21 | 4.2 | 10.5 | 6.3 | | 21.0 |
| | 70 | | 21.0 | 28.0 | 18.9 | 67.9 |
| March | 23 | 4.2 | 10.5 | 6.3 | | 21.0 |
| | 74 | | 21.0 | 28.0 | 21.0 | 70.0 |
| April | 23 | 4.6 | 10.5 | 6.3 | | 21.4 |
| | 74 | | 21.0 | 28.0 | 21.0 | 70.0 |
| May | 25 | 4.6 | 11.5 | 6.3 | | 22.4 |
| | 77 | | 22.2 | 28.0 | 21.0 | 71.2 |
| June | 25 | 5.0 | 11.5 | 6.9 | | 23.4 |
| | 78 | | 22.2 | 29.6 | 21.0 | 72.8 |

stagger, but there is little point in view of the simple nature of the profile.

**c. Direct labour** – all paid during the month in which it occurs.

**d. Stock change** – this is not a cash item and is not included in the forecast.

**e. Overheads** – these are all paid during the month following receipt of the relative invoice with the exception of bank charges amounting to £3,000 in December and June, paid during the month in which they arise.

**f. Depreciation** – not a cash item and therefore excluded.

**g. Capital expenditure** – the company has decided to undertake no major investment expenditure during the period but two items of a capital nature must be allowed for: the sale of a car for £1,000 during December 1978 and hire purchase repayments of £250 per month, excluding interest which is accounted for in other expenses being a profit and loss item which commenced in January 1978.

**h. VAT** – this item was not included in the operating budget because it does not normally affect profitability directly, but it must be shown in the cash plan where its incidence may have far-reaching repercussions. These may be favourable or detrimental, depending on the nature of the business. *XL Engineering* charge VAT on their home sales, but not their exports. They pay VAT on all expenditure, apart from direct labour and 50 per cent of selling, distribution and administrative costs. They settle with Customs and Excise once a quarter on the last day of September, December, March and June. All amounts are at the standard rate of 8 per cent. The company are normally owed money by Customs and Excise because their exports are zero-rated.

In the cash flow forecast that follows, for the sake of ease of understanding, the amount of VAT due is calculated on the actual cash receipts and payments during the quarter. In practice, the position is slightly more complicated because the tax is actually accounted for at what is known as the 'tax point' – usually the date of the invoice or the day of receipt or despatch of the goods.

This information enables the company to draw up a full cash plan. This is shown in Figure 2. (In order to continue the example used in Chapter 8 it should be assumed that the forecast is being prepared during September 1978. The company's overdraft limit is £80,000.)

## 10.4. USING THE CASH PLAN

**The company**

The uses of a cash flow forecast so far as the managers of a business

*Figure 2*

XL Engineering cash flow forecast for twelve months ending 30.6.79

(All figures in '000s)

| | July | August | Sept. | Oct. | Nov. | Dec. | Jan. | Feb. | March | April | May | June | Total |
|---|---|---|---|---|---|---|---|---|---|---|---|---|---|
| **Receipts** | | | | | | | | | | | | | |
| Debtors — home | 17.3 | 17.5 | 18.0 | 18.6 | 19.1 | 20.1 | 21.7 | 22.7 | 22.7 | 23.1 | 24.2 | 25.3 | 250.3 |
|   — export | 52.1 | 53.0 | 54.5 | 56.5 | 59.5 | 61.5 | 65.1 | 67.9 | 70.0 | 70.0 | 71.2 | 72.8 | 754.1 |
| Sale of asset | | | | | | 1.0 | | | | | | | 1.0 |
| Total receipts (A) | 69.4 | 70.5 | 72.5 | 75.1 | 78.6 | 82.6 | 86.8 | 90.6 | 92.7 | 93.1 | 95.4 | 98.1 | 1,005.4 |
| **Payments** | | | | | | | | | | | | | |
| Direct materials | 43.2 | 43.2 | 43.2 | 40.5 | 37.8 | 67.5 | 97.2 | 97.2 | 97.2 | 72.9 | 48.6 | 51.3 | 739.8 |
| Direct labour | 5.0 | 5.0 | 5.0 | 5.0 | 5.0 | 5.0 | 5.0 | 5.0 | 5.0 | 5.0 | 5.0 | 5.0 | 60.0 |
| Production costs | 2.2 | 2.2 | 2.2 | 1.1 | 1.1 | 10.8 | 10.8 | 10.8 | 10.8 | 3.2 | 3.2 | 4.3 | 62.7 |
| Selling & distribution costs | 5.2 | 5.2 | 5.2 | 5.2 | 5.2 | 6.2 | 6.2 | 6.2 | 6.2 | 8.3 | 8.3 | 10.4 | 77.8 |
| Administrative costs | 6.2 | 6.2 | 6.2 | 6.2 | 7.3 | 7.3 | 8.3 | 8.3 | 8.3 | 8.3 | 8.3 | 8.3 | 89.2 |
| Other expenses | — | — | 1.1 | — | 1.1 | 8.6 | 7.6 | 5.4 | 3.2 | 1.1 | — | 4.3 | 32.4 |
| Capital expenditure | 0.3 | 0.3 | 0.3 | 0.3 | 0.3 | 0.3 | 0.3 | 0.3 | 0.3 | 0.3 | 0.3 | 0.3 | 3.6 |
| VAT settlement | | (7.6) | | | (9.6) | | | | (21.7) | | | (10.4) | (49.3) |
| Total payments (B) | 62.1 | 62.1 | 55.6 | 58.3 | 57.8 | 96.1 | 135.4 | 133.2 | 109.3 | 99.1 | 73.7 | 73.5 | 1,016.2 |
| Net cash flow: A—B (Outflow B—A) | 7.3 | 8.4 | 16.9 | 16.8 | 20.8 | (13.5) | (48.6) | (42.6) | (16.6) | (6.0) | 21.7 | 24.6 | (10.8) |
| Opening balance | (50.0) | (42.7) | (34.3) | (17.4) | (0.6) | 20.2 | 6.7 | (41.9) | (84.5) | (101.1) | (107.1) | (85.4) | (50) |
| Closing balance | (42.7) | (34.3) | (17.4) | (0.6) | 20.2 | 6.7 | (41.9) | (84.5) | (101.1) | (107.1) | (85.4) | (60.8) | (60.8) |

*Supporting schedules would show full details where appropriate.*

are concerned are exactly the same as any budget, namely planning, control and co-ordination.

The managers of *XL Engineering* now have a plan showing the cash need of the business. It represents their best estimates of what is most likely to be required. It obviously calls for some action on their part because the maximum debit figure shown is beyond their overdraft limit of £80,000. What options are open to them? Basically two: they can attempt to raise the finance externally, being careful wherever possible to match the type of funds they obtain to the amounts and timings of their needs, and in this case an overdraft facility would appear very suitable as finance is required for current assets and the excess position is only temporary; or they can endeavour to raise cash internally by better management of their cash flow – this aspect is discussed in Chapter 12. This is a key decision point for the business. If the managers defer a decision they may easily find themselves in the crisis situation so familiar to many companies which do not bother to prepare a plan; if they take the wrong decision they may solve the immediate liquidity problem, but only at the expense of profitability. Ironically, the decision is often more difficult for a successful business because its degree of choice is greater and the situation is relatively unfamiliar. A hopelessly inept business does at least have the advantage of being well practised in the art of crisis management.

The forecast is of great value as a means of control. Actual figures should be monitored against the budget, and remedial action taken where necessary to bring the enterprise back on course again. If *XL Engineering* are successful in negotiating a new limit of, say, £110,000 they must obviously take great care to maintain their borrowing within this facility. It will be no good waiting until a telephone call from their branch manager informs them that they are in excess; the time for considered action standing a chance of success may be long past. As with operating budgets, significant variances must be regularly pinpointed and analysed. This is another application of Pareto's Law, in that the amounts to concentrate on are those few which have the greatest effect in absolute terms – with *XL Engineering* the items are sales and direct materials. The variances should be tabulated on a monthly basis using a control report. The root cause of the problem must then be identified and proper corrective action taken. If costs are running away with themselves the sooner this is known the better.

Lastly, the cash plan provides the company with a means of

co-ordinating the activities of all its managers so that they understand the importance of the liquidity problems facing the business
and the part they must play in solving them. It enables the managers
to understand their place in the scheme of things and to appreciate
the value of their efforts. For example, the sales director of *XL
Engineering* now has a clear indication of the importance of his team
meeting their targets for the coming year. As one writer has said:
'It is therefore important that these managers understand the factors
which influence liquidity and cause a particular investment or
source of money to change. Their planning of future activities should
be carried out with full knowledge of the impact their actions will
have on cash, as well as profits and asset utilisation.'[1]

## The banker

A banker must first question the validity of the forecast. He should
ask to see the operating and capital budgets which have been used as
the foundations for the cash plan. If these are not available, how has
the company produced its figures? It should be possible to check the
time delays which the business has calculated; the banker probably
already has some knowledge of the terms of trade in the industry, but
in any event the company can be requested to supply its working
papers.

How realistic are the figures? Is the company being unduly
optimistic in its sales projections? Have all cash items been included?
Have production costs been properly matched with expected sales
after allowing for changes in the stock level? Has the effect of cash
discounts been accounted for? The lending banker should check all
the assumptions which have been made during the production of the
plan. With *XL Engineering* is it reasonable to assume that a cheque
will be received from Customs and Excise in respect of a refund of
VAT during the month in which the return is due? Manifestly not.
This should be pointed out to the customer and the plan suitably
amended. The simplest check of all – the recasting of the form –
should not be overlooked.

The banker will then examine the meaning of the figures. Do they
show that the business has a need for additional finance; if so, how
much, for how long and for what purpose? The plan should provide a
good indication of how cheques will be issued over the period. It
should not be difficult to ascertain the amount being expended on
capital investment and whether this is matched by receipts of a
capital or longer-term nature. It should be equally easy to see the

amount being spent on items of a current nature and this can be related to the fluctuations expected on the banking account. The banker will be anxious to give professional advice to the customer so that the right type of finance can be raised at the best time in appropriate quantities. In the short term a cash flow forecast provides the best basis for this guidance.

Next, the banker should be concerned with variances. Actual figures should be compared with the forecast at regular intervals to ensure that the business is still on course. It should be borne in mind at this stage that the customers will most probably be using the figures for bank borrowing in their books and these will require reconciliation with the balance on the banking account before correct variances can be produced. The customer should be asked to explain the cause of significant variances and outline the steps they are taking to correct the position.

This control aspect is very important. The banker who dismisses cash flow forecasts as a waste of time could be said to be criticising himself for failing to take the trouble to monitor results at regular intervals. To place a cash plan in a desk drawer unexamined for twelve months until the next review of the account is due is like keeping a new car locked in the garage for a similar period. It is not really fair to criticise the performance of either if they are not used.

Some variances will arise solely because the forecast does not show fluctuations that may arise *during* any given month. In certain situations these differences can be large. If, for example, *XL Engineering* issue cheques for all their planned payments during July before they receive any cash from their debtors, the peak overdraft requirement will be £112,100 (£62,100 plus the opening debit balance). In a manufacturing industry such large irregularities are unusual, but in other areas of business they are quite common. They should be allowed for by examining a company's books over a number of months to discover the time of the month when their borrowing peaks and by what amount. If the business is good for an addition to its limit, a percentage can then be added to the facility to allow a reasonable margin. If fluctuations are completely random the position is more difficult. If the business is creditworthy there may be few problems, but if not then the managers of the business will need to exercise all their skills in matching cash flows to available finance.

## 10.5. CASH BUDGETS – A VITAL TOOL FOR BANKERS

There is no doubt in my mind that properly constructed and well-monitored cash flow forecasts overcome many of the shortcomings of traditional tools of lending discussed at the beginning of this book. They provide fundamental help with the three main banking questions:

**a. How much is required?** What could be more precise than a detailed twelve months' cash plan?

**b. What is to be done with the money?** A cash plan shows how cheques will be issued during the period under review. Nothing could provide a more direct indication of the destination of bank finance.

**c. What are the plans for repayment?** In the short term cash plans provide a clear indication. For assessing the longer-term repayment capacity of a business, a different, but complementary, technique needs to be employed. It is called source and application of funds statements and forms the subject of the next chapter.

### Reference

[1] Bishop, S.V.: *Business Planning and Control*. Institute of Chartered Accountants in England and Wales, 1966.

### Further reading

Hartley, W.C.F.: *Cash: Planning, Forecasting and Control*. Business Books, 1976.

CHAPTER 11

# Planning for Liquidity II – Statements of Source and Application of Funds

## 11.1. INTRODUCTION

It is tempting to leave this subject out of this book; it can be argued that it is not strictly within the area of management accounting and, more to the point, there is no general agreement on the best method of presentation of the figures or even the exact meaning of some of the terms commonly used. However at the risk of adding to the confusion, it seems right to include a few words since these statements usually contain something of value to lending bankers and they are now much more frequently encountered following the publication of the Accounting Standards Committee's *Statement of Standard Accounting Practice No. 10* (SSAP 10).[1] This standard called for statements of source and application of funds to be annexed to all financial accounts for business enterprises with a turnover or gross income of £25,000 or more per annum with effect from 1 January 1976.

The basic idea is that for any given period a statement of source and application of funds should provide a link between the initial balance sheet, the closing balance sheet and the profit and loss account running between the two dates. If balance sheets can only reveal a 'frozen' picture of the financial structure of a business at a moment in time, whilst the profit and loss account relates only to items of revenue and expenditure (it does not, for example, show purchases of a capital nature) there would appear to be some value in producing a statement that shows the nature and amount of the funds that became available during the year and how they were used by the managers of the business. This statement in no way replaces the balance sheet or profit and loss account, but should be looked upon as an additional report which draws selected information from these other documents in such a way as to show the overall flow of funds from the beginning to the end of the accounting period. Put more formally it is 'a financial statement which shows the external and internal sources from which funds have been obtained to finance a business during a given accounting period, and the manner in which the funds have been deployed'.[2]

Ignoring the areas of ambiguity for a moment, it seems best to start with some examples of how the statements may be compiled since, in essence, the complicated sounding name of this technique disguises a very simple idea.

## 11.2. SOME EXAMPLES

Turning to a specific example, Figure 1 shows the balance sheets for *ABC Co.*, as at the end of two consecutive financial years. The net movement in the individual assets and liabilities has been calculated and shown in a separate column. Certain information from the profit and loss accounts for the two years has also been included.

Figure 1 provides all the information that is needed to produce a statement of source and application of funds for the company. Remember that the aim of such a statement is to represent the flow of funds during the year and not to provide a mere snapshot of the situation which exists at the end of the accounting period.

In completing the statement it is sometimes difficult to decide quickly whether a particular item is a source or an application of funds, especially when the direction of the flow changes over several balance sheets. The simple rules are:

– Funds are provided from two *sources*:

*i* An increase in a liability (e.g. an increase in creditors).

*ii* A decrease in an asset (e.g. a reduction in stock).

– Funds are *applied* in two ways:

*i* A decrease in a liability (e.g. a reduction in a bank overdraft).

*ii* An increase in an asset (e.g. an increase in debtors).

No items should be included in the statement unless an actual transfer of funds has taken place. Thus, depreciation should be added back to net profits before tax as it is a charge which involves no movement of funds.

Various formats have been used for funds flow statements over the years and the different styles attract their own disciples. SSAP 10 contains various methods of presentation – all very similar in layout – but these are only included for general guidance and 'other methods of presentation may equally comply with the accounting standard'.[3] It seems sensible here to follow the basic format suggested by the accounting standard but it should not be assumed that this represents the only possible layout, or even the most desirable.

*Figure 1*

## Balance sheets for ABC Co. 1976/77

(All figures in '000s)

| | 31.12. 1976 £ | 31.12. 1977 £ | Move- ment £ | | 31.12. 1976 £ | 31.12. 1977 £ | Move- ment £ |
|---|---|---|---|---|---|---|---|
| Creditors | 25.0 | 35.0 | 10.0 | Debtors | 40.0 | 50.0 | 10.0 |
| Bank | 25.0 | 40.0 | 15.0 | Stock | 35.0 | 45.0 | 10.0 |
| Tax | – | 2.5 | 2.5 | | 75.0 | 95.0 | 20.0 |
| | 50.0 | 77.5 | 27.5 | | | | |
| | | | | Land & buildings | 15.0 | 15.0 | – |
| Capital | 10.0 | 10.0 | – | | | | |
| | | | | Plant & machinery | 5.0 | 15.0 | 10.0 |
| Profit & loss | 40.0 | 42.5 | 2.5 | Fixtures & fittings | 5.0 | 5.0 | – |
| | 100.0 | 130.0 | 30.0 | | 100.0 | 130.0 | 30.0 |

| | 1976 £ | 1977 £ | |
|---|---|---|---|
| Net profit after Tax | 2.0 | 2.5 | |
| | – | 2.5 | (included for the sake of illustration – on the figures shown probably no tax would be payable) |
| Depreciation | 0.6 | 1.5 | |
| Directors' remuneration | 4.5 | 5.0 | |

There is considerable diversity in the methods of presentation currently being used by many public companies and it is wise to look closely at the descriptions given to the various figures before attempting any interpretation.[4]

Using the SSAP 10 format for *ABC Co.*, we produce the following statement.

---

**Statement of source and application of funds for ABC Co. 1976/77**

(All figures in '000s)

| Source of funds | £ | |
|---|---|---|
| Profit before tax | 5.0 | |
| Add depreciation | 1.5 | Does not involve a movement of funds: therefore added back as source |
| Total generated from operations | 6.5 | Often termed 'cash flow from trading'. See comments below |
| **Application of funds** | | |
| Tax paid | Nil | The tax of £2,500 has not yet left the company so it remains in the profit figure as a source of funds |
| Purchase of fixed assets | (11.5) | Again, depreciation is added back |
| | (5.0) | |
| **Increase/decrease in working capital** | | |
| Stocks | 10.0 | An application |
| Debtors | 10.0 | An application |
| Creditors | (10.0) | A source |
| Bank | (15.0) | A source |
| | (5.0) | Decrease in working capital used to finance purchase of fixed assets |

---

Once completed, what does this statement show? Turning back to Figure 1 it can be seen that all the amounts shown in the 'movement' column have been included in some way, thus providing a complete listing of all the funds generated during the year and how they were put to use. Furthermore, the effect on the working capital and cash positions can be quickly seen. In this example, profit before tax plus depreciation only contributed approximately 55 per cent of the increased investment in fixed assets. No funds were generated from other sources such as medium-term loans or share issues for cash and, as a consequence, the working capital position was depleted by £5,000. The business was required to finance this deficit and the statement shows how this was done – part of the bank facility was used directly or indirectly to cover the short fall.

There is obviously nothing startling in these conclusions which could have been reached solely on the basis of the layout of Figure 1, but the transference of the movements to a funds flow statement does highlight the precise extent to which the growth of the business is being financed by short-term creditors rather than long-term injections of capital. It also pinpoints the·changes occurring in net liquid funds.

For a more detailed example, statements can be completed for *XL Engineering* using the balance sheets shown in Chapter 3.

## XL Engineering statements of source and application of funds

(All figures in '000s)

|  |  | 1975-6 £ |  | 1976-7 £ |
|---|---|---|---|---|
| **Source of funds** |  |  |  |  |
| Profit before tax |  | 75.6 |  | 105.0 |
| Add depreciation |  | 6.5 |  | 6.0 |
| Total generated from operations |  | 82.1 |  | 111.0 |
| **Application of funds** |  |  |  |  |
| Tax paid |  | (19.0) |  | (30.0) |
| Purchase of fixed assets |  | (9.1) |  | (2.0) |
|  |  | 54.0 |  | 79.0 |
| **Increase/decrease in working capital** |  |  |  |  |
| Stocks |  | 9.0 |  | 78.0 |
| Debtors |  | 14.0 |  | 38.0 |
| Creditors |  | (29.0) |  | (77.0) |
| Directors' current accounts |  | (14.0) |  | – |
| Movement in liquid funds: |  |  |  |  |
| Cash | 72.0 |  | 40.0 |  |
| Bank | 2.0 | 74.0 | – | 40.0 |
|  |  | 54.0 |  | 79.0 |

These reveal the healthy position expected from an examination of the audited figures. The company has generated sufficient funds to cover its purchases of fixed assets, meet its tax commitments and provide £79,000 of additional working capital in 1976-7. This sum, taken with the extra £77,000 that creditors have provided, has enabled the business to build up its stock and debtor positions without any difficulty and maintain a large surplus cash position.

But what of the future? One major value of this technique is in interpreting a company's forecasts of its financial structure and liquidity needs over the longer term. What, for example, will be the position of *XL Engineering* at the end of the 1979 financial year? To examine this, a projected balance sheet must first be produced.

## XL Engineering balance sheet June 1979 (projected)

| Current assets | £('000s) | |
|---|---|---|
| Cash | — | Cash Flow Forecast shows no surplus cash (Chapter 10) |
| Debtors | 281.0 | (From Chapter 10) |
| Stock | 300.0 | Budgeting for an increase of £50,000 during 1978/79 (From Chapter 8) |
| | 581.0 | |
| **Less current liabilities** | | |
| Bank | 61.0 | (From Chapter 10) |
| Creditors | 97.0 | (From information given in Chapter 10) |
| Hire purchase | 10.0 | |
| Directors' current accounts | 34.0 | |
| Current taxation | 30.0 | |
| | 232.0 | |
| Liquid surplus | 349.0 | |
| **Fixed and other assets** | | |
| Land & buildings | 100.0 | |
| Plant & machinery | 22.0 | |
| Fixtures & fittings | 5.0 | Capital expenditure (assumed) |
| Motor vehicles | 15.0 | |
| | 142.0 | |
| Total net assets | 491.0 | |
| Financed by: | | |
| **Term liabilities** | | |
| Future taxation | 50.0 | |
| **Capital** | | |
| Ordinary | 0.4 | |
| Profit & loss | 440.6 | |
| | 491.0 | |
| Net profit | 47.0 | (From Chapter 8, — budgeting for |
| after Tax | 50.0 | profit before tax of £97,000) |
| Depreciation | 10.0 | (From Chapter 8) |
| Directors' remuneration | 45.0 | |

This projected balance sheet provides the information required to complete a funds flow statement spanning the two years.

## XL Engineering statement of source and application of funds 1977/9 (projected)

| | £('000s) | |
|---|---|---|
| **Source of funds** | | |
| Profit before tax | 144.9 | For two years |
| Add depreciation | 22.0 | £10,000 plus £12,000 assumed for earlier year |
| Total generated from operations | 166.9 | |
| **Application of funds** | | |
| Tax paid | (89.0) | For two years |
| Purchase of fixed assets | (41.9) | |
| | 36.0 | |
| **Increase/decrease in working capital** | | |
| Stocks | 88.0 | |
| Debtors | 79.0 | |
| Creditors | 44.0 | Including HP creditors £10,000 |
| **Movements in liquid funds** | | |
| Cash | (114.0) | |
| Bank | (61.0) | |
| | 36.0 | |

This statement reveals a healthy position so far as the capital structure is concerned. Total funds flow generated from trading has been far in excess of the amount required to finance investment in fixed assets and pay corporation tax. On the current side the position is less certain – although working capital has increased, cash resources have been completely depleted and bank aid has been enlisted to build up stocks and debtors – and further investigation is required to make certain that no important problems have arisen. This might take the form of ratio analysis which is discussed in Chapter 13. The position would, of course, have looked much less healthy for the managers of *XL Engineering* if their newly acquired use of budgeting had not enabled them to plan for adequate profits during 1978-9.

## 11.3. AREAS OF AMBIGUITY

In view of its apparent simplicity, it is a little surprising that some confusion surrounds certain aspects of this useful technique. These areas of ambiguity should not be allowed to cloud the value of funds flow statements, nonetheless they need to be briefly examined as some or all will certainly be encountered in practice.

**a. What should they be called?** The heading of this chapter indicates the name by which these statements are commonly known, but – perhaps because this title is a little long-winded – other names are often heard. 'Funds flow statements' has also been used in this chapter and is fairly descriptive of what is being attempted; more so certainly than 'funds statement' which is used frequently in SSAP 10. This latter term appears to many to be an inadequate abbreviation since almost any financial report produced by a business is a statement of funds and, in addition, it does not attempt to describe the summary of movements which the statements reveal. Unusually, the American term 'statement of changes in financial position' is also not very helpful.

**b. Methods of presentation.** As mentioned earlier, there is no consensus on the best style of presentation. For the benefit of readers who may wish to become more conversant with this technique the accounting standard is reproduced in Appendix 2, but it must be emphasised that this format is only a recommendation and other – perhaps clearer – layouts will regularly be encountered in published accounts.

**c. What are funds?** Interestingly, neither the accounting standard nor the glossary of accounting terms produced by the Institute of Cost and Management Accountants see fit to define this word, yet in practice it is not always used to mean exactly the same thing. For example, one writer suggests that 'the term funds is synonymous with working capital'.[5] Whilst another prefers the view that 'in this context the term funds refers to the whole supply of money and credit which the firm uses to carry on its business'.[6]

This seems to me to be another area where a formal definition is less than helpful, but I prefer the wider of the two quoted suggestions since this includes movements of, inter alia, share capital, debentures and fixed assets.

**d. The difference between 'cash' and 'funds'.** In the funds flow statement for *ABC Co.* (see page 106), the term 'total generated from operations' was used to describe the sum of net profit before tax plus depreciation for the year. In banking circles and elsewhere this same figure is frequently called the 'cash flow from trading'. To my mind this is the most confusing term in common use today since it seems to imply to many people that an amount of cash equivalent to these two items has popped up from nowhere at the end of a financial year and is contentedly residing in some deposit account awaiting the call to be used for paying bank charges, dividends, corporation tax, etc. Usually, nothing is further from reality since in a growing company cash receipts – which should include the profit element – will have been ploughed back as additional working capital and/or used to purchase fixed assets. And depreciation can never be a source of *cash*; otherwise all a business would have to do to increase its cash resources would be to up its depreciation charge for a given period – bankers would be quickly out of business!

Funds then are not necessarily cash. A funds flow statement includes non-cash items; an increase in debtors at the year end because of a credit sale which has reduced the stock figure by a related amount (the figures will not be identical because of the profit element) will appear on a funds flow statement although no movement of cash is involved.

## 11.4. A SIMPLE BUT USEFUL TECHNIQUE

Cash flow forecasts are essentially a short-term technique for plotting planned movements in the cash receipts and payments of a business over relatively short periods. They are extremely useful, particularly to bankers, but they do not provide an easily recognisable picture of the way the overall financial structure of a business changes with time. This is the role of *funds flow statements* which should be looked upon as the second stage of planning for liquidity, they do not replace a cash flow forecast or the balance sheet extract form used by most banks and should be viewed as an additional and complementary aid.

Funds flow statements can be used to forecast over longer periods than a cash plan since less detail is required in their preparation. They can yield much assistance to both banker and customer. As one writer has said, 'Funds Flow Plans . . . take a bit more understanding, but the effort is worthwhile. Without them, efficient financing and financial management are impossible'.[7]

# References and notes

1 *Statement of Standard Accounting Practice No. 10 (SSAP 10): Statement of source and application of funds.* The Institute of Chartered Accountants in England and Wales, July 1975 (see Appendix 1).
2 Definition taken from *Terminology of Management and Financial Accountancy,* Institute of Cost and Management Accountants, 1974.
3 SSAP 10: *op. cit.*
4 Readers who would like to delve further into the intricacies of methods of presentation may care to read Egginton, D.A.: 'Funds Through the Looking Glass'. *Journal of The Institute of Bankers,* December 1977.
5 Goff, W.S.: *Management Accounting for Managers.* Macdonald and Evans, 1975.
6 Rockley, L.E.: *The Meaning of Balance Sheets and Company Reports — a Guide for Non-accountants.* Business Books, 1975.
7 Aydon, C.: *Financing Your Company: a Critical Guide.* British Institute of Management, 1972.

CHAPTER 12

# The Management of Working Capital

## 12.1. AN IMPORTANT RESOURCE

The last two chapters have looked at methods of forecasting the cash needs of a business. The object has been to discover how companies can best gauge the size and nature of their requirements for liquid resources over a future period.

This chapter continues and broadens the liquidity theme by considering the importance of managing the whole of the working capital cycle. The aim is not solely to ensure that cash is generated in sufficient quantities at the right time, but also to extract the fullest use from each short-term resource used in a business – 'Every company should aim to optimise its investment in each stage of the working capital cycle'.[1] This involves planning and controlling all the items which drain or augment liquidity.

There can be little doubt as to the relevance of the subject: over the past few years leading authorities have taken every opportunity to urge businesses of all sizes to help themselves through the difficult times by generating internally as much liquidity as possible. In general, business managers have responded well to these promptings from the touchlines; although admittedly many had little choice after their bankers had refused to sanction yet another excess. This has been a positive gain from the bad times that are still with us to a greater or lesser extent. 'One of the major benefits of the liquidity crisis has been that it has forced many companies to recognise the need to manage their cash flow more carefully and in greater detail'.[2] Many businesses have been amazed at the savings they have been able to scrape together. If it has brought home the message to many of them that this is something they should always have been doing, whatever the general economic conditions, then the gain is large indeed.

It is vital that business managers appreciate that working capital is a valuable resource to be managed as fully as any other asset. This is often not an easy message to sell. Many appear to think that they can cope with the task quite comfortably during a coffee break or when pausing between deals with two large new customers. Some would be amazed to hear that time spent on controlling all current items can be every bit as rewarding as the acquisition of new business, and often more so. This is not to minimise the difficulties, however, which can frequently be complex and frustrating.

The items that need to be controlled are well known to bankers. Most of us have been told of the mysterious operation of the working capital cycle so many times during our training that it scarcely warrants further description here. But for the sake of completeness, the main headings for a manufacturing business are as follows:

Working capital cycle (manufacturing)

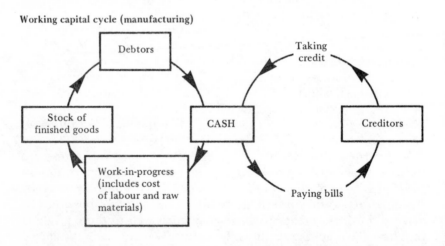

In effect, there are two cycles turning in opposite directions and I like to think of it as an irrigation system with the central cash pool – be this credit balance or overdraft – feeding scarce liquid resources around the fields. This highlights the need for strong central control to ensure that no plants are overwatered whilst others are dying for lack of moisture. It also indicates that the speed of circulation is of no little importance.

The basic questions which require consideration are common to all parts of the cycle: what is the size of the investment? what is it costing? how is it financed? and how can the investment be reduced without harming the firm's ability to meet its objectives?

## 12.2. DEBTOR CONTROL

Very little published information of a practical nature is available on the subject of the control of debtors; yet it is one of the most important areas for concern. A request to a bank for an excess position because funds are due to the company from very good customers whom the directors do not wish to chase, as this might cause offence and thereby lose valuable business, is probably the most frequently encountered excuse in corporate lending. But even if the directors have correctly identified the problem area as debtor control – and in the majority of businesses that I have seen, this is not the case – often much of the blame rests with them because inadequacies in their credit control system have not been identified and remedied.

Many of these deficiencies are not difficult to spot or correct, and bankers can render their customers a great service by encouraging them to do both.

### Aspects to question

#### a. Awareness of the significance of debtors

*i* Has the cost of granting credit been assessed? Some authorities suggest the cost may be as high as 30 per cent of the total of all debtors when interest charges, administrative expenses, legal costs, postage, etc., are taken into account.

*ii* Is it recognised that, assuming the business earns a net profit of 5 per cent (a higher figure than many firms are achieving at present) a bad debt of £5,000 nullifies the profit on £100,000 of sales?

*iii* Has the true cost of discounts been calculated? A $2\frac{1}{2}$ per cent discount for payment within one month when debtors usually pay within 60 days is equivalent to an annual charge of slightly over 30 per cent $(2\frac{1}{2} \times \frac{365}{30} = 30.4)$. Is it worth it? It may be, but only if the business has a pressing need for liquidity.

*iv* Has the amount of working capital needed to finance credit sales been assessed? How much turnover will this support and on what terms?

*v* How many days, on average, does it take to collect one day's credit sales?

*vi* Is it appreciated that if VAT is added to selling prices any debts, outstanding after settlement has been made to Customs and Excise, increase the liquidity problems of the business? And that the VAT on a bad debt is not recoverable from Customs and Excise?

*vii* If no bad debts are being incurred, does this mean the business is too cautious in its credit policy and thereby losing potentially profitable business?

## b. Assessing credit-worthiness

*i* Is the financial standing of all new customers checked before delivery of the first order? There are many sources of information available, including banks, trade references, credit registers, commercial agencies, trade protection societies and local knowledge. Trade references can be particularly helpful especially if the enquiree is telephoned for an answer.

*ii* Are time and amount limits set for each debtor?

*iii* Is the financial standing of customers checked at regular intervals?

*iv* Is it recognised that many salesmen are optimists by nature and may have a vested interest in assuming the best of a customer?

*v* Are the risks inherent in certain trades considered? The rate of business failure is high with jobbing builders and smaller farmers for example. Newly formed firms should also be viewed with greater than average caution.

## c. Sound collection system

*i* Who is responsible for supervising trade credit? Many firms have well-run credit departments that carry out their roles efficiently, but in others it is left to a junior clerk who has little idea of the importance of his task to the success of the business.

*ii* Are invoices sent out promptly? This is an important question. Very few businesses pay on an invoice, but *none* pay before they receive it. The sooner it is sent out the better and this should even be *before* goods are despatched where possible. Businessmen invariably have a plausible-sounding reason for not sending an invoice, e.g. delays in obtaining material prices from stores, but they are usually encouraged to expedite matters when they become aware of the sum their tardiness is costing them.

*iii* Are statements sent out promptly? The statement is usually the first piece of paper that starts debtors even considering the possibility of writing a cheque. Any delay in despatch will automatically extend the period of credit taken.

*iv* Are terms of sale clearly stated on all quotations, price lists, invoices and statements?

*v* Does the business have a systematic collection routine which is always adhered to? This should include a clearly defined procedure of letters, telephone calls, etc. Far too many managers only start chasing when the debt has been outstanding for many months. Debtors should be asked politely, but firmly, to pay the amounts they owe at regular intervals. In most cases, the fear many businessmen have of upsetting good customers is more imagined than real. And in any event, there should come a time when customers who only settle their accounts after excessively long time lags are no longer thought of as desirable. Delivery to these customers should then cease. Frequently goods continue to be supplied when on the basis of past experience there is obviously little or no chance of payment being made for them.

*vi* Is the ratio of debtors to sales monitored regularly? This is discussed again in Chapter 13.

*vii* Is a debtor ageing analysis regularly completed? This simple form, shown below can provide invaluable help to many smaller firms and takes very little time to complete.

*viii* Has credit insurance been considered?[3] This is not cheap but it may be worth it in some circumstances.

*ix* Would factoring be advantageous for the business? Once again, many businessmen may think of this as an expensive service. But there are occasions when it repays its cost many times over purely in efficiency of debt collection.

## ABC Co. Debtor ageing analysis (£1,000 and over)

| Debtor | Age 1 month | 2 months | 3 months | Total | Remarks |
|---|---|---|---|---|---|
| Smith Bros. | 5,050 | 1,000 | | 6,050 | 2nd letter |
| R.S. Lead | 6,000 | | | 6,000 | |
| Brown & Son | | 7,500 | 2,200 | 9,700 | 3rd letter |
| Blacks | 7,200 | | | 7,200 | |
| R.V. Jones | | 10,500 | 2,000 | 12,500 | Telephone |
| S. & S. | 2,600 | | 8,400 | 11,000 | Telephone No more work |
| Rawlins | | 3,700 | | 3,700 | |
| Green & Co | | | 4,000 | 4,000 | 3rd letter |
| Total | 20,850 | 22,700 | 16,600 | 60,150 | |
| Percentage | 34.7 | 37.7 | 27.6 | 100 | |

## d. Chasing delinquent debtors

*i* The telephone can prove an effective means of obtaining payment. Is it used?

*ii* Have a series of letters been devised which get progressively tougher?

*iii* Has the use of debt collectors been considered?

*iv* Are personal visits ever undertaken?

*v* Having threatened legal action, does the business instigate proceedings? Obviously steps should be taken to ensure that the cost of such action will be rewarded by results.

*vi* Are debts written off before collection costs far outweigh their value? All businesses must take some degree of risk and this inevitably means that some money will be lost.

## e. Investigating queries

*i* Some debts are not paid promptly because of queries on the account. Are these investigated quickly or put to one side to gather dust until someone has the time to examine them?

*ii* Are they placed in a logical sequence so that large amounts and bills with very minor queries are dealt with first?

These procedures may sound very time consuming. But, as with most aspects of management, it is a matter of establishing priorities. In most businesses with an inadequate debtor control system the cost of improvement is amply rewarded. None of the techniques are difficult and bankers (who, after all, are not without experience in these matters!) can provide considerable guidance and assistance to their customers, 'The management of debt is an important part of financial management . . . (It) is essentially a practical problem'.[4]

## 12.3. STOCK MANAGEMENT

For many firms, particularly those in the manufacturing sector, stock represents a large proportion of their current assets. It can be a heavy user of working capital and must be a prime target for attention in any business concerned to maintain its profitability and liquidity at optimum levels and make the most effective use of the scarce resources at its disposal. It is an area of considerable importance to bankers because expensive money tied up in stock is usually a drain on the profits of an enterprise until the stock is sold. In addition, the rate of stock turnover can have a marked effect on the short-term repayment capacity of a business.

Stock management is not the same as storekeeping, which is a term used to refer to the physical supervision of the storage of stock and the issuing of items as and when required subject to the procedures operated by the firm.

Rather is stock management a managerial function involving planning and controlling a company's investment in its holding of stock of all types. And it is often forgotten that working capital can be absorbed by types of stocks other than the familiar pattern of raw materials, work-in-progress and finished goods. Spare parts for sophisticated machinery and specialised moulds and dies are examples of expensive items which may be carried in the stock figure and ignored by company managers as being of a capital nature and therefore representing 'sunk' costs. This can present a misleading picture, especially if ratios are used to analyse the stock position.

Stock management is important because the lack of it can cost a business a great deal of money and harm its ability to meet its obligations as they fall due. A survey of the garage trade produced by the National Economic Development Office[5] contained the startling information that the average cost of holding spare parts valued at £100 for one year was £65! In the garages examined, the effect on net profit would have been exactly the same whether an average business had increased its turnover by £26,000 or reduced stocks by a mere £1,000. Admittedly, these figures were compiled on the basis of fully absorbed costs and cannot be applied to situations where small amounts of stock are being added or subtracted at the margin, but they nevertheless serve to illustrate the need for sound control.

## a. Conflicting objectives

The major difficulty facing any financial manager responsible for an effective stock management policy is that he will be forced to tread a path between the individual objectives of various areas of the business. These separate aims are often in conflict:

*i* **Customer service** – the ideal situation for a sales force is one where they are able to satisfy all requests from customers immediately. They want stocks of all finished products in the company's range to be readily available at all times as this will give them a competitive edge in the market.

*ii* **Production efficiency** – the production manager will want sufficient stocks of raw materials, bought-in components and partly finished goods to be on hand at all times to ensure maximum efficiency of production. He abhors any situation where his men and machines stand idle because of a stock shortage.

*iii* **Economic forecasts** – many businesses engage in pre-emptive buying when they expect the prices of their main raw materials to increase. This tendency has been seen frequently over the last few years when high rates of inflation alone have caused large upward revisions of prices at regular intervals over a wide range of commodities and components. Forward purchasing may be an excellent policy for well-managed concerns that are able to forecast market trends accurately, quantify the extra costs involved in carrying higher levels of stock and pass this expense on to the ultimate consumer. But few companies are in this position. Many base their decisions on nothing more than a vague feel for the market or a wish to join the ranks of those few, but vociferous, entrepreneurs who have made a fortune out of holding a commodity for a short period of time. The results are sometimes disastrous.

*iv* **Minimum investment** – the financial manager realises that the holding of stock is a non-interest-earning investment that is expensive to maintain and a drain on precious working capital. His aim is to keep the total of the company's financial resources tied up in stock down to the minimum practical level.

## b. Evidence of problems

These conflicting aims often result in an imbalance appearing in a company's stock position. This can become apparent in various ways:

*i* **Poor customer service** – one of the early warning signs comes from consumers. They will react to late deliveries or poor standards by complaining, or withdrawing their business. The sales force will not be slow in bringing the problem to the attention of their fellow managers in other areas of the business. Salesmen are often the most articulate servants of a business, however, and this can cause the problem to be overstated. Also the difficulties may not stem from poor stock policies.

*ii* **Excessive production inefficiency** – the symptoms of this problem are usually obvious to even an untrained observer: production lines come to a halt because of the lack of one small component and the labour force stand idle; the percentage of rejected items and returned goods increase; excessive work-in-progress clutters the workshop and contributes to the inefficiency; backlogs of orders develop because of shortages; and there is a general air of unease and uncertainty.

*iii* **Low rate of stock turnover** – as has already been discussed. This is important because stock is an expensive burden carried by a business and only contributes to profits and cash flow when it is sold and paid for. The measurement of the rate of stock turnover is discussed in the next chapter.

*iv* **Substantial excess or obsolete holdings** – businessmen are often reluctant to admit even to themselves that such a situation exists. 'It will all go eventually' is a frequently heard comment, without a thought being given to the cost of carrying the goods until they are converted into cash. This will often negate any profit which may have been expected when the items were purchased.

*v* **Substantial shortages or 'shrinkage'** – these often go unnoticed or unchecked and can lose a business a great deal. It will sometimes cost more to police stock than a business can hope to regain from savings, but at least a proper recording system will tell management how much needs to be recovered in their costing schedules to recoup pilferages. This may seem unfair to the consumer, but prices would be higher if full security measures were to be introduced, and competitive pressure should serve to prevent the worst abuses.

*vi* **General lack of information** – the business that is able to tell its bankers little other than the story that its stock is vastly under- or over-valued for tax purposes presents a *prima facie* case of poor stock management.

## c. Remedying problems

Stock management in many larger companies is a job which should rightly be the province of experts. The analysis and correction of stock problems in these companies can be extremely complex, involving the use of sophisticated techniques and advanced mathematical models.

There are, however, aspects of the subject which are not so difficult in concept:

*i* **Basic decisions** – these are simply: how much to order – what is the best quantity to purchase at a time, bearing in mind the conflict of aims within the business and the discounts which may be obtained for quantity; when to order – what level of stock of a particular item can the business afford to drop to before re-ordering; is a safety stock required – this is linked to the previous question and is important for those items where a complete lack of stock would cause widespread disruption; and what stock items are significant?

*ii* **Aids to decision making** – once again, there is no substitute for well constructed objectives and a properly thought out plan. Any major decision on stocks must accord with the overall aims of the business.

Next, a business should single out for attention the most significant items, and Pareto's Law can be very helpful in this connection. This suggests that businesses should concentrate on those relatively few items of stock that make up a large percentage of the value of the total holding. This reduces the cost of control but achieves effective management over the bulk of the working capital captured by stock. I have seen the case of a repair business that carried over 200,000 different items of stock. Their service to customers was excellent, but profits were negligible because of the high cost of carrying such a vast range of spare parts. Many of the items were cheap and easy to obtain; effective control over them would have cost a great deal and brought little financial benefit. But some parts were expensive and scarce and the simple management system that was introduced to maintain them at an appropriate level was quickly rewarded.

A refinement of Pareto's Law is the 'ABC System'. This recognises that within the 80 per cent of less significant items some will be more important than others either because of increased usage or through higher cost and should probably be controlled more stringently. In a typical business the system might operate as follows:

| Class | No. of parts % | Usage/value % | Type of control |
|-------|-------|-------|-------|
| A | 15 (i.e. a little less than Pareto's 20 per cent) | 60 | Close control Good records Maintain safety stock Review frequently |
| B | 25 | 25 | Good control, but not as close as A Review less frequently |
| C | 60 | 15 | Little control Few reviews |

This system needs to be used with discretion, giving more weight to high cost items than those with a high usage. All Class A stocks should be ordered carefully at the right time and in the most economic quantity. The most desirable maximum and minimum stock levels should be carefully assessed, taking into account lead times (the period between despatch of an order and receipt of the goods) and the future pattern of production. Ratios can be produced for each category and targets set in terms of the number of days' or weeks' stock on hand at any given time.

Stock records can provide a good indication of those products that are selling and those that are not. This, coupled with a marginal costing analysis to indicate contributions, can lead to a reduction in the spread of the product range involving consequent reductions in stock. This can actually produce an increased turnover because more resources can be directed to the remaining products which the business has already decided produce a greater contribution.

### d. XL Engineering Co.

Typical of many companies of its size, *XL Engineering* was seriously overstocked and had no real stock management policies. Expensive components were bought months before work was due to start on a job; frequently without anyone looking in one of its many small store sheds to see if the item was already being held. Poor production planning often meant that jobs expected to earn good margins and having expensive components already held in stock were not given priority through the factory. Although holding far too much stock in total, certain important parts were in short supply and were often missing at a vital stage in the production. Stock turn had been decreasing over the years and there were numerous discrepancies between the records and the actual stock.

It was considered perfectly feasible for the business to reduce its stock figure by 30 per cent over one year from the date of the survey by using the ABC System. The total holding had been valued at £212,000 at the end of the 1977 financial year and so, assuming that the stock would realise at least its book value, a dramatic improvement in liquidity should be seen as the £63,000 is released, first as debtors and finally as cash. Assuming an interest rate of 10 per cent the saving in borrowing costs alone will be over £6,000. The inclusion of other costs could be expected to double this figure at least.

### 12.4. CREDITOR CONTROL

Often completely overlooked, this can be an important area. Paying creditors involves an outflow of working capital and if this is in short supply then they will need to be kept waiting for their money. Even so, there are good reasons why a business should have a policy for paying its creditors:

**a.** In the final analysis, creditors are the people who force a company into liquidation. Those who start legal action may not always be the ones who have previously shouted loudest. It is easy to pay all smaller amounts promptly only to find that no money is left to meet the larger amounts, and it is normally the larger creditor who institutes proceedings.

**b.** A business may be crippled by the failure of a supplier. There is little point in nursing your own working capital position so carefully as to destroy the only source of a vital component.

**c.** Taking credit from suppliers may represent a very expensive way of borrowing money if valuable cash discounts are lost.

Any firm should keep a check on what it owes. It is easy to accept extended credit from suppliers only to discover after a few months that the total debt has reached an alarming figure. A form similar to that suggested for debtor ageing can be used effectively for this purpose.

Companies short of cash should not overlook the possibility of joint ventures with businesses enjoying a more liquid position or co-operation from a supplier who may be content to hold stock to be drawn off in small lots as required provided he has a guaranteed production run.

## 12.5. CONCLUSION

Sound management of working capital is vital to the success of a business. A properly controlled position may not always assist the profitability of a business, but it will invariably help its chances of staying solvent.

As one writer has said 'The rules for staying solvent are really very simple, but rarely observed in full . . .

(1) Budget your cash flow
(2) Control your debtors
(3) Control your creditors
(4) Control your stocks
(5) Do not over borrow
(6) Do not over invest in fixed assets'[6]

# References

[1] Sizer, J.: 'What we Should be Doing About the Company Liquidity and Profitability Crisis'. *Management Accounting*, October 1975.

[2] *Ibid.*

[3] Handley, P.: 'Credit Insurance'. *Journal of The Institute of Bankers*, October 1975.

[4] Samuels, J.M. and Wilkes, F.M.: *Management of Company Finance*. 2nd ed. Nelson, 1975.

[5] Economic Development Committee for Motor Vehicle Distribution and Repair: *Profitable Stock Management:- a brief guide for motor traders*. National Economic Development Office, 1971.

[6] Wood, E.G.: *Bigger Profits for the Smaller Firm*. Business Books, 1972.

CHAPTER 13

# Ratio Analysis

## 13.1. INTRODUCTION

This chapter examines the strengths and weaknesses of ratios as a means of analysing company performance. It discusses those ratios well known to bankers which show trends in liquidity, and others concerned with profitability which are perhaps less frequently encountered. The value of a ratio to highlight repayment capacity is also examined briefly.

Ratios can provide great help to management in the planning and control of a business, but they must be used with caution and with a full understanding of the limitations of the figures. Nowhere is this caveat more important than in the field of ratio analysis: any businessman or banker who believes that an enterprise can be fully successful solely by maintaining a few key ratios at a certain level is, in my opinion, very mistaken. Ratios can never be a substitute for good management. But they can help to inform it. This is their strength and more should not be expected of them.

A simple but effective test of whether a ratio is being used properly is to ask the manager producing it to explain its value in clear, easy-to-understand terms. If he has difficulty in doing so, it probably means either that he is as mystified as you are or he is using the ratio incorrectly: 'It should, however, be a golden rule for all users, and particularly occasional users, to ask themselves the question "What is the precise significance of this ratio?" '[1]

Because they are so important, the basic rules for calculating and using ratios are discussed next.

## 13.2. USING RATIOS

At the risk of introducing aspects of the subject which may be thought too elementary, the following points should be noted:

**a.** A ratio is a means of comparing one figure with another. It is particularly helpful when used to describe a situation where the individual figures have little meaning viewed in isolation. For example, to say that a car travels from A to B in two hours has little value as an indicator of the speed of the vehicle. But as soon as it is known that the distance involved is 60 miles then the speed ratio – 30 miles per hour – is precise and simple to understand.

**b.** A ratio is made up of two parts, a numerator and a denominator and can never be more correct than the least accurate constituent. Ratios calculated to four decimal places can take on a spurious air of accuracy and should be viewed with caution. It is often difficult, however, to decide which figure is the least accurate and why.

**c.** The figures should be related to each other to the extent that they can provide a comparison that has some meaning. It is difficult to imagine that a figure for elephants per machine hour could ever have much value as a tool for management, yet equally meaningless ratios are regularly encountered in practice.

**d.** Many financial ratios make use of audited accounts and these may suffer from all the shortcomings discussed in previous chapters.

**e.** The same comparison can be expressed in different ways and this may contain pitfalls for the unwary. The commonly encountered sales to stock ratio can be expressed in at least four ways –

| | | | |
|---|---|---|---|
| $\dfrac{Stock}{Sales}$ | $= \dfrac{£212,000}{£690,000}$ | $= 0.31$ | (stock turnover ratio) |
| $\dfrac{Sales}{Stock}$ | $= \dfrac{£690,000}{£212,000}$ | $= 3.25$ | (number of times stock turned over) |
| $\dfrac{Stock \times 365}{Sales}$ | $= \dfrac{£212,000 \times 365}{£690,000}$ | $= 112$ days | (days in which stock turned over once) |
| $\dfrac{Stock \times 100}{Sales}$ | $= \dfrac{£212,000 \times 100}{£690,000}$ | $= 30.7\%$ | (stock turnover percentage) |

The figures are taken from the 1977 accounts of *XL Engineering Co. Ltd* (contained in Chapter 3).

**f.** The ratio of sales to stock can also be used to illustrate another difficulty: wherever possible both figures in a ratio should be measured and valued in the same terms. This cannot happen when the stock figure is taken from a balance sheet showing values at the close of the financial year and sales are taken from a profit and loss account having accumulated over the period. Sales are valued at the selling prices set from time to time, whereas stock is entered at either the cost or net realisable value at the year end (whichever is lower). A more realistic ratio is obtained by comparing *average* stock with sales. (Or better still, average stock with the *cost of sales* during the period if this can be ascertained.)

As with many smaller companies no weighted average of twelve months' stock figures is available for *XL Engineering*. An approximation can be made by halving the total of the opening and closing figures, although with some businesses this will provide a very inaccurate result. This produces the following ratios:

| | | |
|---|---|---|
| Average stock | $\dfrac{£134,000 + £212,000}{2}$ | = £173,000 |
| Stock turnover ratio | $\dfrac{£173,000}{£690,000}$ | = 0.25 |
| Number of times stock turned over | $\dfrac{£690,000}{£173,000}$ | = 4.0 |
| Days in stock | $\dfrac{£173,000 \times 365}{£690,000}$ | = 91.5 days |
| Stock turnover percentage | $\dfrac{£173,000 \times 100}{£690,000}$ | = 25.1% |

As can be seen, the ratios thus produced are significantly different from the figures in **e.** above (little credence should be given to the actual ratio itself, however; much more important to the banker is the general trend over a period of years).

**g.** Ratios should be interpreted against some sort of standard. This is discussed later.

### 13.3.  RATIOS TO ASSESS LIQUIDITY

In the main, ratios to assess liquidity are well known to bankers and need not be examined in any depth here.
The usual ratios are:

**a.  The Current Ratio   =**

$$\frac{\textbf{Current Assets}}{\textbf{Current Liabilities}}$$

This ratio indicates the ability of a business to meet its current obligations as they fall due. The underlying idea is that stock and debtors are turned into cash which becomes available to meet short term liabilities.

### b. The Acid Test Ratio =

$$\frac{\text{Cash + Debtors + Readily Realisable Investments}}{\text{Current Liabilities}}$$

The current ratio pays little heed to the nature of the current assets and their degree of liquidity. A business maintaining high levels of stock of all types in comparison with its remaining current assets is not so well placed to meet its immediate commitments as a business with a higher percentage of more liquid funds. The 'acid test' ratio overcomes this difficulty by relating current liabilities to the 'quick' assets of cash, debtors and readily realisable investments. Obviously, an important factor to examine behind this ratio is the underlying quality of the debtors.

### c. The Borrowing Ratio =

$$\frac{\text{Total Borrowings}}{\text{Net Worth}}$$

This ratio gives an indication of 'gearing'; a term frequently used but often not defined, or expressed in the form of a ratio. There is some argument amongst bankers over the items to be included in the liabilities which make up this ratio. To my mind, the important thing is a consistent approach so that trends can be highlighted in a realistic way, but I prefer to use the term 'net worth' to mean the shareholders' stake in the business and 'total borrowings' to mean all borrowed monies from any source regardless of term.

A business is said to be highly geared when the proportion of borrowed money is high in relation to net worth and low geared when the opposite applies. A highly geared position need not indicate that a business is in a precarious state or vice versa. Much will depend on the nature of the industry and general economic conditions. A good wholesaler with a rapid turnover of stocks will normally be able to operate satisfactorily with a much higher gearing than, say, a manufacturer of expensive capital equipment where added value is high and manufacturing periods long. The wholesaler has little need to tie up capital in fixed assets and can quickly convert his current assets to cash in case of need.

**d. Average Credit Granted** =

$$\frac{\textbf{Average Debtors}}{\textbf{Sales}}$$

The importance of debtor control was raised in Chapter 12 and this ratio can be a useful means of knowing when closer attention to the area is required and in the setting of targets for managers. Average debtors over the period under review is to be preferred to the figure at the year end because it relates like with like.

The ratio is most helpful when expressed in terms of days, weeks or months and this is achieved simply by multiplying the ratio by 365, 52 and 12 respectively. For *XL Engineering*, assuming average debtors of £183,000 in the 1973/4 year (opening and closing positions added and halved – although in practice, it is better to obtain regular figures from the books), the ratios are as follows:

| | |
|---|---|
| Credit granted in days | $= \dfrac{£183,000}{£690,000} \times 365 = 96.8$ |
| „    „    in weeks | $= \dfrac{£183,000}{£690,000} \times 52 = 13.8$ |
| „    „    in months | $= \dfrac{£183,000}{£690,000} \times 12 = 3.2$ |

The use of *XL Engineering* as an example illustrates the need to look behind the figures. It will be remembered that a large part of the company's turnover is sold abroad and it is, therefore, much more realistic and more useful to management to segregate debtors into home and export and produce separate ratios for each.

**e. Average Credit Taken** =

$$\frac{\textbf{Average Creditors}}{\textbf{Purchases}}$$

Reference was made in Chapter 12 to the value of maintaining a continuing check on the creditor position. This ratio may be expressed in time periods in the same way as that for credit granted, but there is one additional problem: businesses sometimes include borrowings from a wide range of sources in their creditor figure and care must be exercised to ensure that only those items which relate to the purchases figure are included.

## f. The Working Capital Ratio   =

$$\frac{\text{Working Capital}}{\text{Sales}}$$

I include this simple ratio which is well covered in most of the banking textbooks only because it seems underutilised. It quickly provides a rough and ready calculation of the likely amount of additional working capital required by a given increase in sales.

Calculating the ratio for *XL Engineering* from their 1977 figures:

$$\frac{\text{Working Capital}}{\text{Sales}} = \frac{\text{Current Assets} - \text{Current Liabilities}}{\text{Sales}}$$

$$= \frac{£528,000 - £220,000}{£690,000} = \frac{£308,000}{£690,000} = 0.45 \text{ or } 45\%$$

Thus on the face of things the Company would require an additional £450 of working capital for every £1,000 of additional sales.

Many other factors need to be taken into account of course, but the ratio presents a useful starting point for a discussion of a business' liquidity needs, particularly where some expansion is contemplated.

## 13.4.  RATIOS TO ASSESS PROFITABILITY

A full set of ratios to assess the success or failure of a business in the area of profitability is less commonly used by bankers. Simple calculations on the gross and net profit positions are not without some value, but they do little to identify the root cause of poor performance or to indicate the use a business is making of the assets at its disposal. For assistance in these areas the aid must be enlisted of ratios which relate sales, profit and capital employed. These three factors can be bound together in a simple, but extremely useful, way:

| 1 | 2 | 3 |
|---|---|---|
| $\dfrac{\text{Profit}}{\text{Capital Employed}}$ | $= \dfrac{\text{Sales}}{\text{Capital Employed}}$ | $\text{x } \dfrac{\text{Profit}}{\text{Sales}}$ |

There is nothing magical about this equation – the figures for Sales in ratios 2 and 3 can be cancelled out to leave ratio 1 – but it does enable a business to separate the components which make up the return it is achieving on its resources into a rate of turnover of those resources (ratio 2) and a straight return on sales (ratio 3). The significance of this is that an improvement in the rate of use of resources will produce as good a return to a business as an equivalent improvement in its overall profit margin, and can be much easier to achieve in the market place. Many businessmen, like most bankers, ignore this concept which is another expression of certain aspects of the cost-volume-profit relationship covered in Chapter 7.

Once again, there are problems of definition, with both profit and capital employed being open to calculation in a number of different ways. There is no right answer and much depends on the needs of the user, but the aim should always be consistency. For the manager of a business, a definition of capital employed is to be preferred which involves the inclusion of all tangible resources employed in earning a profit, i.e. total assets less intangible and fictitious, less current liabilities; and a definition of profit which includes only those benefits arising from the trading operations of a business, i.e. net profit before taxation and interest charges, excluding items of a capital or non-trading nature. Bankers may find more acceptable those definitions which relate more closely to figures readily available in the audited accounts.

Ratios 2 and 3 can be further divided to produce a pyramid of ratios. This is not difficult to construct and can be very helpful in pinpointing areas of unsatisfactory performance.

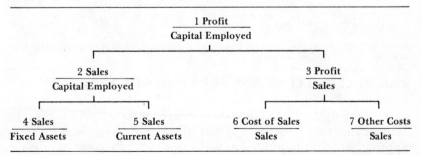

Further sub-division is possible and in many cases desirable: current assets can be separated into debtors and stocks of raw materials, work-in-progress and finished goods; and cost of sales can be split into direct materials, direct labour and other direct expenses.

Figure 1 tabulates the ratios for *XL Engineering* from the actual results for 1975-77, and the forecast for 1979 projected in the balance sheet shown in Chapter 11. Interestingly the rate of asset turnover has increased from 1977 to 1979 in a satisfactory manner, but the improvement has been more than offset by poorer profit margins – down from 0.15 to 0.09. Ratios 6 and 7 cannot be computed from the information given to date in this book but it seems likely that an increase in direct costs is the cause of the poorer performance. This confirms the results of earlier analysis and leads the way for the managers of the business to break down ratio 6 into its constituent parts for a more detailed examination. Lastly, it should be noted that some of the ratios shown in the pyramid indicate liquidity as well as profitability, e.g. current assets to sales.

---

*Figure 1*

XL Engineering Co. Ltd

Summary of Ratios

| Ratio | 1975 | | 1976 | | 1977 | | 1979 (Projected) | |
|-------|------|---|------|---|------|---|------|---|
| 1. | $\dfrac{60,000}{314,500}$ | $= 0.19$ | $\dfrac{75,600}{360,100}$ | $= 0.21$ | $\dfrac{105,000}{430,100}$ | $= 0.24$ | $\dfrac{97,000}{491,000}$ | $= 0.20$ |
| 2. | $\dfrac{584,000}{314,500}$ | $= 1.86$ | $\dfrac{601,000}{360,100}$ | $= 1.67$ | $\dfrac{690,000}{430,100}$ | $= 1.60$ | $\dfrac{1075,000}{491,000}$ | $= 2.19$ |
| 3. | $\dfrac{60,000}{584,000}$ | $= 0.10$ | $\dfrac{75,600}{601,000}$ | $= 0.13$ | $\dfrac{105,000}{690,000}$ | $= 0.15$ | $\dfrac{97,000}{1075,000}$ | $= 0.09$ |
| 4. | $\dfrac{584,000}{123,500}$ | $= 4.73$ | $\dfrac{601,000}{126,100}$ | $= 4.77$ | $\dfrac{690,000}{122,100}$ | $= 5.65$ | $\dfrac{1075,000}{142,000}$ | $= 7.57$ |
| 5. | $\dfrac{584,000}{277,000}$ | $= 2.11$ | $\dfrac{601,000}{372,000}$ | $= 1.62$ | $\dfrac{690,000}{528,000}$ | $= 1.31$ | $\dfrac{1075,000}{581,000}$ | $= 1.85$ |

Note: All profit figures before tax, but *after* all other charges and receipts as details not provided by available information.

---

## 13.5. RATIO TO ASSESS REPAYMENT CAPACITY

A useful addition to the profitability ratios is one that compares earnings with the cost of outside borrowed money, to which can be added capital repayments, if desired. There are a number of different approaches to pinpointing strengths or weaknesses of a business in this area. I prefer a ratio that is easy to calculate and simple to understand:

**Profit (before taxation and interest)**

**Interest charges on outside borrowed money**

This provides a good indication of the margin of safety (or lack of it) in a business' commitments to outside lenders.

## 13.6. COMPARISON OF RATIOS

All of the foregoing leads to the question raised by most small and medium-sized businesses after a discussion on ratios: 'This is all very well, but what *should* our ratios be?'

Unfortunately, there can be no black and white answers to this question. What is right for one industry will be completely wrong for another. Often quite large companies survive and prosper on ratios that are well outside the norms quoted by most authorities. Bankers are often heard to suggest that the ideal Current Ratio is 2:1, but many large international companies operate successfully on figures where the margin of safety is much smaller than this.

It is possible, however, to make comparisons which serve to provide standards of varying degrees of usefulness:

**a. Trends within the business** – this is often the most valuable means of comparison because all the relevant factors of importance are known. It is easy to ensure that all ratios are determined using standard criteria, and this is an important consideration if comparisons are to be valid. If forecasting methods are in operation, internal comparisons will often identify problems before they actually occur.

**b. Comparisons with other businesses** – generally speaking, this is of less value because it is difficult to make certain that another company is similar in terms of size, products, markets and objectives and that all ratios have been completed using common criteria. However, it should not be ignored as a possible avenue of help and the necessary information may be obtained from many sources:

*i* Audited figures of similar firms. Any ratios produced will, however, suffer from all the deficiencies of the figures on which they are based.

*ii* Financial publications. The *Financial Times* and *Investors' Chronicle* regularly publish selected ratios on certain industries, but, once again, the statistics suffer the disadvantage of having been obtained from published company information.

*iii* Trade associations, employers' organisations and other representative bodies. This information ranges in value from very useful to offering extremely limited assistance. Much depends on the methods used to produce the figures and the depth of the base from which they are drawn. Most of this information is not available to non-members.

*iv* Special studies. Government or industry sponsored reports occasionally appear and provide useful figures for comparison. Alternatively, a firm can instigate its own study using an independent organisation such as the Economist Intelligence Unit.

*v* No list of possible sources of comparative ratios would be complete without mentioning the British Institute of Management's Centre for Inter-Firm Comparison which operates an excellent system designed to ensure as far as possible that all ratios are computed to a common pattern.

But outside comparisons can never be of more than limited value. At the end of the day, the only proper judgement is whether the ratios indicate that the business is meeting the aims set for it: 'Before considering what ratios the chief executive should examine, the long-term objectives of the firm must be defined'.[2]

## 13.7. CONCLUSION

It cannot be stressed too strongly that the shortcomings of ratio analysis are important. The manager who rushes into action merely on the strength of a series of ratios is being very foolhardy. The strength of ratios is in indicating where to look; the exact nature of the problem and the type of remedial action to be taken are matters for managerial judgement.

### References

[1] Bevan, K.W.: *The Use of Ratios in the Study of Business Fluctuations and Trends.* The Institute of Chartered Accountants in England and Wales: General Educational Trust, 1966.
[2] Westwick, C.A.: *How to Use Management Ratios.* Gower, 1973.

CHAPTER 14

# Management Reports

## 14.1. INTRODUCTION

Managing a business successfully is far from easy. This much should be clear from what has been covered so far. Managers must attempt to use the resources at their disposal to achieve optimum results – that level where men, machines, materials and money are being fully used to produce the best return consistent with the short and longer-term aims of the business. The task would not be a simple one even if the internal and external factors exerting influence over the fortunes of an enterprise remained unchanged over periods of time, and it is made highly complex by the dynamic nature of all businesses where relationships between the physical and financial aspects are constantly altering.

Consider, for example, the sales figure, which a banker often sees merely as a total in a trading account. A businessman will be forced to view this item in a much more detailed way. He will need to know how individual products are faring, which salesmen are performing inadequately, how sales are split geographically, if colours and packaging require changing, and so on. Place these considerations alongside the many other changing influences and the size and nature of the difficulties facing business managers become very apparent. As few have the wisdom of Solomon, most businesses fail to achieve their full potential, by margins both large and small.

Such complexities are not eased by a lack of information. An obvious sounding statement, perhaps, but a message ignored by many companies nonetheless. A great number of businessmen have little or no relevant data on which to base their decisions; many suggest that extra paperwork is an additional expense they neither need nor can afford, and in any case they are much too busy handling queries and pushing up turnover. They run the business by some imagined 'feel' or sixth sense and often appear busy because they are continually being called upon to solve crisis situations which need never have arisen if appropriate control information had been available at the right time. The laws of chance will ensure that some businessmen with no more than a nose for a bargain will survive and prosper, but the odds are stacked against them; for every one that succeeds, many will fail. And, importantly, the more successful the business becomes, the greater the odds against it.

This chapter is about management information: the need for it and the features of good reports. It cannot cover every type of information document used by businesses because that would run to many volumes. Instead it concentrates on the more useful examples, including a regular statement of trading results which all but a few businesses should find helpful.

## 14.2. WHAT IS GOOD INFORMATION?

The most important feature any information report should possess is usefulness. It must help the managers of a business to plan and control their operations more effectively or it has no value. Many large companies have masses of information produced since time immemorial the purpose of which has long since been forgotten, if one ever existed. In most small businesses managers have little idea of the type of information they might need and make this an excuse for inactivity. The solution for big business is often to bring in a new broom on a temporary or permanent basis, while the smaller firm should be encouraged – by bankers and others – to start gradually with forms and systems that are quick to complete and immediately useful in the running of the business. The first rule, then, is relevance.

Secondly, good reports should be up-to-date even if only reasonably accurate. It is much better that a monthly profit and loss report should appear on the managing director's desk on the fifth day of the succeeding month correct to the nearest thousand pounds than two months after the event correct to the nearest penny. By the same token, there is nothing to be gained by bursting a blood vessel and bringing the works to a halt just to produce the information, say, one day earlier on the fourth of the month. The criterion is: what is reasonable? The cost of producing the information at a certain time to a given degree of accuracy must be balanced against the benefits to the firm.

Next, reports should be frank and honest. This is one of the strengths of management accounting: the figures need not be doctored for outside consumption; it does not have to adhere to any requirements established externally; its purpose is to help managers manage and its ability to do this is hampered by false assessments. It also demands some ability on the part of the people preparing the reports. The figures will only be as realistic as the skill of the compiler allows. However, this should normally not present a major problem if the management is prepared to look around – there are accountants, consultants and other outside advisers available to assist for a fee. Some of the clearing banks offer a free service designed specifically to help their smaller customers in this area; and excellent proprietary systems are available from companies who provide free advice on the installation and use of their products.

Lastly, presentation is important. A good meal tastes better when it is attractively served and the same is true of management information. It should be legible and easy on the eye. It should be structured logically so that key points are highlighted. It should be as concise as possible; too much detail will blur the message. The layout should be changed as little as possible; users dislike constantly being forced to find their way around new forms. The report should facilitate comparison: most figures assume a greater meaning when they are set against others to which they are related.

## 14.3. TYPES OF INFORMATION

It has already been mentioned that reports can take almost any form and cover a wide variety of topics depending upon the requirements of a business. The most important ones (and perhaps the only ones a managing director will see) are those concerned with profitability, liquidity, volume and productivity. Reports under these headings will usually be of great importance to the success of a company and therefore of considerable interest to lending bankers.

**a. Profitability** – It must be true that the ability to extract up-to-date information on profitability is of prime importance to business managers and bankers. To await the production of audited accounts results in a delay which some firms may not be able to afford and the shortcomings of such figures severely limit their value. Regular monthly or quarterly profit figures should be the answer to many a banker's prayer so long as they can be produced reasonably promptly with an acceptable degree of competence.

How difficult is this information to produce and what form should the report take? It would be foolish to pretend that it is always an easy procedure, although most of the difficulties will centre around one or two headings. The table below shows an example of a monthly report on the previous month's trading and the accompanying schedules provide supporting information (see pages 141-142).

## ABC Co. Ltd

## Monthly profit & loss account

|  | This period | | Year to date | |
|---|---|---|---|---|
|  | Budget £ | Actual £ | Budget £ | Actual £ |
| Sales | 16,000 | 15,600 | 32,000 | 30,500 |
| Less | | | | |
|    Cost of sales | 8,500 | 8,400 | 16,500 | 16,300 |
| Gross profit | 7,500 | 7,200 | 15,500 | 14,200 |
| Less overheads | 3,750 | 4,000 | 7,500 | 7,450 |
| Net profit | 3,750 | 3,200 | 8,000 | 6,750 |
| Tax @, say, 50% | 1,875 | 1,600 | 4,000 | 3,375 |
| Profit after tax | 1,875 | 1,600 | 4,000 | 3,375 |

The heading which presents the greatest difficulty to most businesses is that for stock. A poor assessment under this heading will normally have a significant effect on the net profit figure and firms should strive to achieve a reasonable measure of accuracy, although this will need to be weighed against the cost of the work involved. In certain businesses, particularly those where the stock items are few in number, it is not an onerous task to check and value the stock at regular intervals, especially if an efficient stock control system is in operation. For companies with larger numbers of items, Pareto's Law can be adapted to obtain sound valuations for the few items which make up the bulk of the total in monetary terms, to which can be added a percentage for the remainder that are physically checked much less frequently. Alternatively, some businesses have a costing system which readily identifies the value of stock.

If these methods fail or are not appropriate it is often acceptable to estimate closing stock levels by assuming a gross profit percentage. In a fairly stable business which is not under strong pressures to expand or contract and where there is no marked seasonality, the relation of gross profit to sales remains fairly constant. Once this figure has been assumed, the calculation of the closing stock is a simple mathematical exercise as it becomes the only unknown figure in the trading account.

A lesser problem arises with some overheads that are paid at irregular intervals. These should not be charged in one lump against profit in the month during which payment falls due, but spread over all the months in which their benefit is felt.

*Schedule 1*

## ABC Co. Ltd

## Cost of sales analysis

|  | This period | | Year to date | |
|---|---|---|---|---|
|  | Budget £ | Actual £ | Budget £ | Actual £ |
| Opening stock | 25,000 | 24,500 | 25,000 | 24,500 |
| Add purchases | 8,500 | 8,300 | 16,500 | 16,200 |
|  | 33,500 | 32,800 | 41,500 | 40,700 |
| Less closing stock | 25,000 | 24,400 | 25,000 | 24,400 |
| Cost of sales | 8,500 | 8,400 | 16,500 | 16,300 |

*Schedule 2*

## ABC Co. Ltd

## Sales analysis

|  | This period | | Year to date | |
|---|---|---|---|---|
|  | Budget £ | Actual £ | Budget £ | Actual £ |
| By product |  |  |  |  |
| Product A | 5,000 | 5,200 | 10,000 | 9,500 |
| Product B | 4,000 | 3,800 | 8,000 | 8,500 |
| Product C | 7,000 | 6,600 | 14,000 | 12,500 |
|  | 16,000 | 15,600 | 32,000 | 30,500 |
| By location |  |  |  |  |
| Area 1 | 6,000 | 5,600 | 12,000 | 11,500 |
| Area 2 | 10,000 | 10,000 | 20,000 | 19,000 |
|  | 16,000 | 15,600 | 32,000 | 30,500 |

*Schedule 3*

## ABC Co. Ltd

## Purchases analysis

|  | This period | | Year to date | |
|---|---|---|---|---|
|  | Budget £ | Actual £ | Budget £ | Actual £ |
| **By product** | | | | |
| Product A | 2,500 | 2,400 | 5,000 | 4,900 |
| Product B | 2,000 | 1,900 | 4,000 | 3,900 |
| Product C | 4,000 | 4,000 | 7,500 | 7,400 |
|  | 8,500 | 8,300 | 16,500 | 16,200 |
| **By location** | | | | |
| Area 1 | 3,500 | 3,000 | 6,500 | 6,300 |
| Area 2 | 5,000 | 5,300 | 10,000 | 9,900 |
|  | 8,500 | 8,300 | 16,500 | 16,200 |

*Schedule 4*

## ABC Co. Ltd

## Overheads analysis

|  | This period | | Year to date | |
|---|---|---|---|---|
|  | Budget £ | Actual £ | Budget £ | Actual £ |
| Salaries & wages | 2,500 | 2,600 | 5,000 | 5,000 |
| Rent & rates | 500 | 450 | 1,000 | 800 |
| Insurance | 50 | 50 | 100 | 150 |
| Vehicle expenses | 200 | 300 | 400 | 450 |
| Miscellaneous | 500 | 600 | 1,000 | 1,050 |
|  | 3,750 | 4,000 | 7,500 | 7,450 |

All estimates should err on the conservative side, i.e. revenues should be underestimated, costs should be overallowed. It is preferable to be better off than you think you are. But the tolerances should be kept within reasonable bounds otherwise the picture will become so distorted that it loses all value.

The most desirable system of profit reporting (and the one illustrated in the table on page 140) is one that links with a firm's budgeting process so that actual figures may be compared with those planned. Where this is not practical, monthly figures for current profitability should still be produced as they will constitute an important aid to management for most businesses.

**b. Liquidity** – The techniques of cash flow forecasting have already been examined and the monitoring of 'actual' against 'budget' represents an invaluable form of management reporting. In addition, there may be occasions when further reports on cash flows are required for specific aspects of a company's operations. For example, a large contract making heavy demands on working capital may need to be controlled separately, although it must still have a place in the overall plan.

**c. Volume** – Most businesses have a good flow of information on the overall path of their sales, but many do not segregate from the total figure those items which are of most significance.

This presents yet another application for Pareto's Law. Generally speaking, most of a company's turnover will come from a few of its customers and a small number of products in its range. Obviously, sales statistics and production data should be concentrated on these customers and products.

**d. Productivity[1]** – Productivity is a subject discussed by all manner of people, but few suggest ways in which it can be assessed and controlled. Even the experts cannot agree on a standard method of measurement.

Basically, productivity may be defined as the relationship between output and resources. It is similar in concept to the ratio of sales to capital employed mentioned in the last chapter. Higher productivity need not be indicative of a greater volume of production. It might mean that fewer resources have been used to produce the same quantity of goods. In practical terms, it involves measuring actual output obtained from labour and machines and comparing the result with what could or should have been achieved.

The chapter on costing emphasised the need to produce accurate measures of labour and machine efficiency in order to calculate appropriate rates for the recovery of overheads. These are not figures which should be guessed at (although they often are, with disastrous results) or obtained from a trade association. They should be calculated for each business so that they can be used to produce realistic estimates and plans.

By way of an example, the form in Figure 1 shows a labour analysis report which is capable of being applied in a wide range of industries.[2]

*Figure 1*

| ABC Co. Ltd | | | | | | | | |
|---|---|---|---|---|---|---|---|---|
| Labour analysis report | | | | | | | | |
| – Labour utilisation by department | | | | | | | | |
| For week ended: | | | | | | | | |
| Department | Productive A | Hours | | | | | Total B | Utilisation % $\dfrac{(A)}{(B)} \times \dfrac{100}{1}$ |
| | | Non-productive | | | | | | |
| | | Waiting for Materials | Machine Breakdown | Etc. | Etc. | Total | | |
| | | | | | | | | |
| | | | | | | | | |
| | | | | | | | | |
| | | | | | | | | |
| Totals | | | | | | | | |

## 14.4. RELEVANCE TO BANKERS

The reports discussed serve as good indicators of the state of health of a business. As such, they are of considerable value to bankers who should ask to see as many as they feel happy to assess and discuss. In my experience, all but a very small number of business customers are happy to send copies of the more important reports to their bankers. Most are delighted that a bank should be taking such a close interest in their affairs.

The complete absence of any of the reports indicates, in my view, poor management. No business can be said to be effectively managed when it lacks the knowledge on which to base decisions. Bankers can be of much assistance to customers who fall into this category by making suggestions about the most suitable forms of management information.

### References and notes

[1] For the sake of simplicity and brevity, this section suggests that the terms productivity and efficiency are identical in meaning. I believe this to be permissible within the content of this book. The distinction between the two can be explored with further reading if desired and most textbooks on management accounting contain a fuller explanation.

[2] I acknowledge the help given by Arthur Andersen & Co. in the preparation of this form.

CHAPTER 15

# Some Closing Thoughts

I began this book with some comments which represented my personal views. Having endeavoured since then to keep my feet fairly firmly placed on the bedrock of established management accounting principles and their relevance to the lending banker, I hope I may be forgiven for straying once again into less clearly defined territory in this brief concluding chapter.

To begin by re-emphasising two points made in the introduction: first, I have neither the ability nor the desire to render obsolete those established banking principles that have stood the test of time. The basic canons of lending have their roots so firmly embedded in practical commonsense that it would be foolish to deny them their undiminishing importance. As was stated at the outset, the point of the series of articles on which this book is based was to examine whether certain other techniques could provide useful supplementary information to the credit analyst. Any banker who feels that he has sufficient facts constantly at his fingertips to deal with most corporate lendings that cross his desk will certainly have stopped reading long before now. The shortcomings of certain traditional aids to lending mentioned at the beginning need not be reiterated, but they should provide a powerful argument in favour of an examination of additional sources of help for anyone prepared to explore them.

Secondly, I do not for one moment wish to pretend that a knowledge of management accounting provides the key to unlock every lending problem. Apart from any other consideration, many of our small and medium-sized businesses will require many years of persuasion and counselling before they will admit to seeing any benefit in monthly reports, budgeting tools and the like. But if we are prepared to concede that we often lend on a shallow base of information then what other discipline is there available to turn to for assistance? Only management accounting offers techniques that, when sensibly used in the proper hands, ought to provide some help in opening up the dark areas which exist in most smaller companies.

## 15.1. A CHECKLIST

Although it may not have been readily apparent, all of the areas discussed are linked in some way: well produced cash flow forecasts are dependent upon a good profit budgeting process which in turn relies on sound costing systems. Other links may be less obvious, but each aspect of management accounting should help to build up an overall view of a business. No chart can be produced to illustrate fully this interdependence since it would contain a vast network of lines joining each heading to almost every other heading. All that can be offered is a checklist which, whilst acting primarily as a type of aide memoire, may also help to join the threads of the subject together. Such a listing is provided in Appendix 3 and is merely intended as a guide. It does not pretend to be fully comprehensive and is capable of amendment to suit individual preferences.

## 15.2. PEOPLE MATTER MOST

None of this is intended to suggest that the character and personality of the people who run businesses are of little practical importance. Quite the opposite: the best management information will be of little benefit to business managers who continually ignore it, preferring instead to base their decisions on some imagined hunch or sixth-sense. Of course, most new businesses start in this way. Smaller companies rarely begin their progress to success simply because their directors are well versed in sophisticated management techniques. Usually it is quite the opposite: they survive through their ability to complete the quick deal, and they grow because their size provides them with a degree of flexibility in meeting customer needs which often cannot exist with the larger business. The danger in accepting this general picture is twofold: for every one small firm that can be counted as a success many more are failures, and – just as important – the profitable expanding concern often realises far too late that the seat-of-the-pants style of management which provided the initial impetus needs supplementing with a sound system of planning and control if the business is not to run all the risks of a ship without proper course or charts.

Management accounting systems can be introduced gradually. A business that may be frightened off by talk of budgeting and capital investment appraisal may instead be perfectly happy to attempt a small amount of profit and loss reporting, perhaps on a quarterly or six-monthly basis at first. Management information must be seen to be of some use to the people who run a business; unless this is so there will be little incentive to continue its production. The systems should be kept as simple as possible, sufficient for the needs of the role asked of them and no more.

As has been mentioned before, when assessing the worth of a company's management should not the quality of the available information base be ranked alongside the traditional judgements of honesty and endeavour? Business is about people, and people matter most. But without more than their fair share of luck, business managers can only be as good as the information on which they base their decisions.

## 15.3. THE BANKER'S ROLE

In this book I have endeavoured to pinpoint particular areas where, in my opinion, a banker may offer help and guidance. Many readers may feel that such assistance is neither desirable nor possible: undesirable because it is not part of a banker's role since his duty is to judge the quality of the final performance and not to become involved in the rehearsal rooms, impossible because of time constraints which appear to press on branch bankers more heavily year by year.

So far as the first opinion is concerned there is little more I can say. I can but agree to differ with readers who hold this view. The question of the lack of available time is a different matter: it must be agreed that this is a major area of difficulty. A certain amount can be done by managers, their colleagues in branches and area officials, but I suspect that any real advancement in the use of management accounting as an aid to lending depends on a restructuring of systems and procedures in the typical clearing bank. Surely we are soon to enter the era of the skilled corporate lender? The manager who, although based in line banking, will have no responsibility for branch administration and be supported by a small team of well-trained credit analysts – possibly younger men and women who will not have spent their first five years learning exclusively the mysteries of accounting machines and counter books. Beyond this will be a team in area or head office who will possess the time and training to take a business proposition apart and put it back together again in a constructive way.

Our business customers deserve nothing less. And I suspect that as time goes by those of us who earn our living in a clearing bank will prosper on nothing less.

# APPENDIX 1

## PRESENT VALUES OF £1

from 1 to 15 years ahead at rates of interest from 5% to 20%

| Years ahead | 5% | 6% | 7% | 8% | 9% | 10% | 11% | 12% |
|---|---|---|---|---|---|---|---|---|
| now | 1.000 | 1.000 | 1.000 | 1.000 | 1.000 | 1.000 | 1.000 | 1.000 |
| 1 | .952 | .943 | .935 | .926 | .917 | .909 | .901 | .893 |
| 2 | .907 | .890 | .873 | .857 | .842 | .826 | .812 | .797 |
| 3 | .864 | .840 | .816 | .794 | .772 | .751 | .731 | .712 |
| 4 | .823 | .792 | .763 | .735 | .708 | .683 | .659 | .636 |
| 5 | .784 | .747 | .713 | .681 | .650 | .621 | .593 | .567 |
| 6 | .746 | .705 | .666 | .630 | .596 | .564 | .535 | .507 |
| 7 | .711 | .665 | .623 | .583 | .547 | .513 | .482 | .452 |
| 8 | .677 | .627 | .582 | .540 | .502 | .467 | .434 | .404 |
| 9 | .645 | .592 | .544 | .500 | .460 | .424 | .391 | .361 |
| 10 | .614 | .558 | .508 | .463 | .422 | .386 | .352 | .322 |
| 11 | .585 | .527 | .475 | .429 | .388 | .350 | .317 | .287 |
| 12 | .557 | .497 | .444 | .397 | .356 | .319 | .286 | .257 |
| 13 | .530 | .469 | .415 | .368 | .326 | .290 | .258 | .229 |
| 14 | .505 | .442 | .388 | .340 | .299 | .263 | .232 | .205 |
| 15 | .481 | .417 | .362 | .315 | .275 | .239 | .209 | .183 |

| Years ahead | 13% | 14% | 15% | 16% | 17% | 18% | 19% | 20% |
|---|---|---|---|---|---|---|---|---|
| now | 1.000 | 1.000 | 1.000 | 1.000 | 1.000 | 1.000 | 1.000 | 1.000 |
| 1 | .885 | .877 | .870 | .862 | .855 | .847 | .840 | .833 |
| 2 | .783 | .769 | .756 | .743 | .731 | .718 | .706 | .694 |
| 3 | .693 | .675 | .658 | .641 | .624 | .609 | .593 | .579 |
| 4 | .613 | .592 | .572 | .552 | .534 | .516 | .499 | .482 |
| 5 | .543 | .519 | .497 | .476 | .456 | .437 | .419 | .402 |
| 6 | .480 | .456 | .432 | .410 | .390 | .370 | .352 | .335 |
| 7 | .425 | .400 | .376 | .354 | .333 | .314 | .296 | .279 |
| 8 | .376 | .351 | .327 | .305 | .285 | .266 | .249 | .233 |
| 9 | .333 | .308 | .284 | .263 | .243 | .225 | .209 | .194 |
| 10 | .295 | .270 | .247 | .227 | .208 | .191 | .176 | .162 |
| 11 | .261 | .237 | .215 | .195 | .178 | .162 | .148 | .135 |
| 12 | .231 | .208 | .187 | .168 | .152 | .137 | .124 | .112 |
| 13 | .204 | .182 | .163 | .145 | .130 | .116 | .104 | .093 |
| 14 | .181 | .160 | .141 | .125 | .111 | .099 | .088 | .078 |
| 15 | .160 | .140 | .123 | .108 | .095 | .084 | .074 | .065 |

Reproduced by kind permission of Industrial and Finance Corporation Limited from their publication *Appraising capital Investment Proposals* by R.W. Powell.

# APPENDIX 2

## STATEMENT OF STANDARD ACCOUNTING PRACTICE NO. 10
## STATEMENTS OF SOURCE AND APPLICATION OF FUNDS (SSAP 10)

*(Issued July 1975)*

*The object of this statement is to establish the practice of providing source and application of funds statements as a part of audited accounts and to lay down a minimum standard of disclosure in such statements.*

## PART 1 – EXPLANATORY NOTE

**1** The profit and loss account and the balance sheet of a company show, inter alia, the amount of profit made during the year and the disposition of the company's resources at the beginning and the end of that year. However, for a fuller understanding of a company's affairs it is necessary also to identify the movements in assets, liabilities and capital which have taken place during the year and the resultant effect on net liquid funds. This information is not specifically disclosed by a profit and loss account and balance sheet but can be made available in the form of a statement of source and application of funds (a 'funds statement').

**2** The funds statement is in no way a replacement for the profit and loss account and balance sheet although the information which it contains is a selection, reclassification and summarisation of information contained in those two statements. The objective of such a statement is to show the manner in which the operations of a company have been financed and in which its financial resources have been used and the format selected should be designed to achieve this objective. A funds statement does not purport to indicate the requirements of a business for capital nor the extent of seasonal peaks of stocks, debtors, etc.

**3** A funds statement should show the sources from which funds have flowed into the company and the way in which they have been used. It should show clearly the funds generated or absorbed by the operations of the business and the manner in which any resulting surplus of liquid assets has been applied or any deficiency of such assets has been financed, distinguishing the long term from the short term. The statement should distinguish the use of funds for the purchase of new fixed assets from funds used in increasing the working capital of the company.

**4** The funds statement will provide a link between the balance sheet at the beginning of the period, the profit and loss account for the period and the balance sheet at the end of the period. A minimum of 'netting off' should take place as this may tend to mask the significance of individually important figures; for example, the sale of one building and the purchase of another should generally be kept separate in a funds statement. The figures from which a funds statement is constructed should generally be identifiable in the profit and loss account, balance sheet and related notes. If adjustments to those published figures are necessary, details should be given to enable the related figures to be rapidly located.

**5** Funds statements should, in the case of companies with subsidiaries, be based on the group accounts. They should reflect any purchases or disposals of subsidiary companies either *(a)* as separate items, or *(b)* by reflecting the effects on the separate assets and liabilities dealt with in the statement, so that the acquisition of a subsidiary company would be dealt with as an application of funds in acquiring the fixed assets (including goodwill) of that subsidiary and as a change in working capital. In either case, in the interests of clarity, it will generally also be necessary to summarise the effects of the acquisition or disposal by way of a footnote indicating, in the case of an acquisition, how much of the purchase price has been discharged in cash and how much by the issue of shares. Examples of the alternative treatments are shown in examples 2 and 3 (see pages 154-155).

**6** A funds statement should form part of the audited accounts of a company.

**7** Although this accounting standard is for application to all enterprises other than small enterprises with a turnover or gross income less than £25,000 per annum, consideration should nevertheless be given to the particular circumstances of such enterprises with a view to furnishing the funds statement wherever it is desirable.

## PART 2 – DEFINITION OF TERMS

**8** *Net liquid funds:* cash at bank and in hand and cash equivalents (e.g. investments held as current assets) less bank overdrafts and other borrowings repayable within one year of the accounting date.

## PART 3 – STANDARD ACCOUNTING PRACTICE

**9** This accounting standard shall apply to all financial accounts intended to give a true and fair view of financial position and profit or loss other than those of enterprises with turnover or gross income of less than £25,000 per annum.

**10** Audited financial accounts should, subject to paragraph 9 above, include a statement of source and application of funds both for the period under review and for the corresponding previous period.

**11** The statement should show the profit or loss for the period together with the adjustments required for items which did not use (or provide) funds in the period. The following other sources and applications of funds should, where material, also be shown:
*(a)* dividends paid;
*(b)* acquisitions and disposals of fixed and other non-current assets;
*(c)* funds raised by increasing, or expended in repaying or redeeming, medium- or long-term loans or the issued capital of the company;
*(d)* increase or decrease in working capital sub-divided into its components, and movements in net liquid funds.

**12** Where the accounts are those of a group, the statement of source and application of funds should be so framed as to reflect the operations of the group.

### Date from which effective

**13** The accounting practices set out in this Statement should be adopted as soon as possible and regarded as standard in respect of financial statements relating to accounting periods beginning on or after 1st January 1976.

The examples that follow are for general guidance and do not form part of the Statement of Standard Accounting Practice.

*The methods of presentation used are illustrative only and in no way prescriptive and other methods of presentation may equally comply with the accounting standard. The format used should be selected with a view to demonstrating clearly the manner in which the operations of the company have been financed and in which its financial resources have been utilised.*

Example 1

**Company without Subsidiaries Ltd**
**Statement of Source and Application of Funds**

|  | This year | | | Last year | | |
|---|---|---|---|---|---|---|
|  | £'000 | £'000 | £'000 | £'000 | £'000 | £'000 |
| **Source of funds** | | | | | | |
| Profit before tax | | 1,430 | | | | 440 |
| Adjustments for items not involving the movement of funds: | | | | | | |
| Depreciation | | 380 | | | | 325 |
| **Total generated from operations** | | 1,810 | | | | 765 |
| | | | | | | |
| **Funds from other sources** | | | | | | |
| Issue of shares for cash | | 100 | | | | 80 |
| | | 1,910 | | | | 845 |
| | | | | | | |
| **Application of funds** | | | | | | |
| Dividends paid | (400) | | | (400) | | |
| Tax paid | (690) | | | (230) | | |
| Purchase of fixed assets | (460) | | | (236) | | |
| | | (1,550) | | | | (866) |
| | | 360 | | | | (21) |
| **Increase/decrease in working capital** | | | | | | |
| Increase in stocks | 80 | | | 114 | | |
| Increase in debtors | 120 | | | 22 | | |
| (Increase) decrease in creditors — excluding taxation and proposed dividends | 115 | | | (107) | | |
| Movement in net liquid funds: | | | | | | |
| Increase (decrease) in: | | | | | | |
| Cash balances | (5) | | | 35 | | |
| Short-term investments | 50 | 45 | 360 | (85) | (50) | (21) |

Example 2

## Groups Limited
## Statement of Source and Application of Funds
(based on the accounts of the Group and showing the effects of acquiring a subsidiary on the separate assets and liabilities of the Group)

|  | This year | | | Last year | | |
|---|---|---|---|---|---|---|
|  | £'000 | £'000 | £'000 | £'000 | £'000 | £'000 |
| **Source of funds** | | | | | | |
| Profit before tax and extraordinary items, less minority interests | | 2,025 | | | | 2,610 |
| Extraordinary items | | 450 | | | | (170) |
|  | | 2,475 | | | | 2,440 |
| Adjustments for items not involving the movement of funds: | | | | | | |
| Minority interests in the retained profits of the year | | 25 | | | | 30 |
| Depreciation | | 345 | | | | 295 |
| Profits retained in associated companies | | (40) | | | | – |
| **Total generated from operations** | | 2,805 | | | | 2,765 |
| **Funds from other sources** | | | | | | |
| Shares issued in part consideration of the acquisition of subsidiary* | | 290 | | | | – |
| Capital raised under executive option scheme | | 100 | | | | 80 |
|  | | 3,195 | | | | 2,845 |
| **Application of funds** | | | | | | |
| Dividends paid | | (650) | | | (650) | |
| Tax paid | | (770) | | | (970) | |
| Purchase of fixed assets* | | (660) | | | (736) | |
| Purchase of goodwill on acquisition of subsidiary* | | (30) | | | – | |
| Debentures redeemed | | (890) | | | – | |
|  | | | (3,000) | | | (2,356) |
|  | | | 195 | | | 489 |
| **Increase/decrease in working capital** | | | | | | |
| Increase in stocks* | | 120 | | | 166 | |
| Increase in debtors* | | 100 | | | 122 | |
| Decrease in creditors—excluding taxation and proposed dividends* | | 75 | | | 17 | |
| Movement in net liquid funds: | | | | | | |
| Increase (decrease) in cash balance* | (35) | | | 10 | | |
| Increase (decrease) in short-term investments | (65) | | | 174 | | |
|  | | (100) | | | 184 | |
|  | | | 195 | | | 489 |

**\*Summary of the effects of the acquisition of Subsidiary Limited**

| Net assets acquired | | Discharged by | |
|---|---|---|---|
| Fixed assets | 290 | Shares issued | 290 |
| Goodwill | 30 | Cash paid | 60 |
| Stocks | 40 | | |
| Debtors | 30 | | |
| Creditors | (40) | | |
|  | 350 | | 350 |

Example 3

## Groups Limited
## Statement of Source and Application of Funds
(based on the accounts of the Group and showing the acquisition of a subsidiary as a separate item)

| | £'000 | This year £'000 | £'000 | £'000 | Last year £'000 | £'000 |
|---|---|---|---|---|---|---|
| **Source of funds** | | | | | | |
| Profit before tax and extraordinary items, less minority interests | | 2,025 | | | 2,610 | |
| Extraordinary items | | 450 | | | (170) | |
| | | 2,475 | | | 2,440 | |
| Adjustments for items not involving the movement of funds: | | | | | | |
| Minority interests in the retained profits of the year | | 25 | | | 30 | |
| Depreciation | | 345 | | | 295 | |
| Profits retained in associated companies | | (40) | | | – | |
| Total generated from operations | | 2,805 | | | 2,765 | |
| **Funds from other sources** | | | | | | |
| Shares issued in part consideration of the acquisition of subsidiary* | | 290 | | | – | |
| Capital raised under executive option scheme | | 100 | | | 80 | |
| | | 3,195 | | | 2,845 | |
| **Application of funds** | | | | | | |
| Dividends paid | (650) | | | (650) | | |
| Tax paid | (770) | | | (970) | | |
| Purchase of fixed assets | (370) | | | (736) | | |
| Purchase of Subsidiary Ltd* | (350) | | | – | | |
| Debentures redeemed | (890) | | | – | | |
| | | (3,030) | | | (2,356) | |
| | | 165 | | | 489 | |
| **Increase/decrease in working capital** | | | | | | |
| Increase in stocks | | 80 | | | 166 | |
| Increase in debtors | | 70 | | | 122 | |
| Decrease in creditors—excluding taxation and proposed dividends | | 115 | | | 17 | |
| Movement in net liquid funds: | | | | | | |
| Increase (decrease) in cash balance* | (35) | | | 10 | | |
| Increase (decrease) in short term investments | (65) | | | 174 | | |
| | | (100) | | | 184 | |
| | | | 165 | | | 489 |

*Analysis of the acquisition of Subsidiary Limited

| Net assets acquired | | Discharged by | |
|---|---|---|---|
| Fixed assets | 290 | Shares issued | 290 |
| Goodwill | 30 | Cash paid | 60 |
| Stocks | 40 | | |
| Debtors | 30 | | |
| Creditors | (40) | | |
| | 350 | | 350 |

APPENDIX 3

## CHECKLIST FOR CORPORATE CUSTOMERS

This list is offered in the hope that it may be of some value to bankers who have little corporate lending experience. It does not pretend to be fully comprehensive and it can be amended to suit individual preferences.

### 1. History of business
○ How old is the business?
○ Are founders still connected?
○ Steady growth or erratic progress?
○ Any major problems in the past which are likely to recur?
○ At first glance is the company young and thrusting (and possibly lacking a sense of caution and responsibility), or old and unambitious (not necessarily a criticism; such businesses often make very good customers).

### 2. Ownership
○ Who owns the business?
○ Do owners have full/partial control over the day-to-day running?
○ Identify any inter company holdings.
○ Will present owners be prepared to leave profits in business during difficult times?
○ Have owners any further liquid assets to introduce in case of need?
○ What will be the consequences of the death of one/all owners?
○ Are personal guarantees of owners necessary?

### 3. Corporate objectives (see Chapter 4)
○ What are the general objectives of the directors?
○ Are these: quantified / ambitious / attainable / flexible / appropriate?

O Do they include at least one from this list: profitability / liquidity / product mix / market position / productivity?

## 4. Management
O Ages.
O Responsibilities.
O Background, qualifications and experience.
O All able to grow with business?
O Any gaps? (Think of key areas: general management, sales, production, finance.)
O Succession.

## 5. Labour resources
O Numbers and type: male / female; full-time / part-time; skilled / unskilled; union / non-union.
O Adequacy / quality / availability: all right to meet objectives?
O Senior and key employees: what are ages, how easy to replace, should they be insured?
O Wages: how do they compare with area; details of bonus schemes / overtime / shift rates / fringe benefits.
O How controlled and supervised?
O Relations with management. Good communications?
O Absenteeism / turnover.
O Productivity / performance / attitude to job.

## 6. Premises
O Location / age.
O Freehold / leasehold.
O Adequate space: short term / medium term.
O Security of tenure: terms of lease.
O Room and approval for expansion.
O Is layout good?
O What is general condition? Do premises appear suitable for work being carried out?
O Fire regulations observed?
O Other legislation being met?
O Valuation and basis.
O Insurance adequate?

## 7. Plant and machinery
O What are major items: condition and adequacy / when require

replacement / cost of replacement?
- O Owned or leased?
- O Maintenance policy and planning.
- O Depreciation rate policy.
- O Planned expenditure.
- O How is expenditure to be appraised? (see Chapter 9)
- O What is utilisation rate?
- O Any obvious 'white elephants' which could be sold?
- O Percentage of total fixed costs?
- O Insurance adequate?

## 8. Financial resources
- O What lines of credit are available to business including HP and leasing commitments?
- O Are financial resources adequate to meet objectives? Any restraints on growth?
- O Is financial structure sound: gearing / liquidity ratios / mix of finance correct as to term and amount for needs of company?
- O Is management aware of all types of facilities available? Factoring / leasing / discounting / etc.
- O Is repayment capacity adequate?
- O Vulnerability to outside pressures.
- O Profitability: steady or volatile?
- O Capital commitments.
- O Contingent liabilities.

## 9. Products and markets
- O What are major products? Are markets for these products expanding / declining?
- O Is performance of present products closely monitored: sales trend / market share / profitability / contribution?
- O What factors influence demand: price / fashion / delivery dates / quality / seasonality?
- O Which customers are most important: 10 per cent / 20 per cent / 30 per cent of turnover? Have these customers been asked what their buying policy is likely to be in the future?
- O New products planned: what is policy on new products?
- O Are complaints logged?
- O Can products be easily copied / have they been patented?
- O What market research is carried out? How are markets changing?

○ Product range: too wide / too narrow / never examined / properly recorded?
○ 'Make in' or 'buy out' decisions properly thought through?
○ Size of order book: logged by product range / effect on working capital assessed?
○ Wholesaling / distribution / packaging policies right: reviewed regularly?
○ Marketing strategies correct? sales force / method of approach / order processing / geographical areas covered / advertising / right products promoted?
○ Competitors monitored closely?
○ Export policy.

## 10. Purchasing
○ Control and responsibility.
○ Dependent on one / few suppliers?
○ Lead times.
○ Is price sole determinant?
○ Reliability / quality of raw material / component purchases.
○ How often are possible new suppliers examined: are regular quotations obtained? Availability of alternative supplies?
○ Are discounts for quantity obtained? Who decides on order quantity?
○ Who are large creditors; are they sympathetic during periods of temporary cash shortage?
○ Can suppliers carry stock; if so, on what terms?
○ How does business treat its creditors? Does it pay in shouting order or attempt to preserve important sources of supply?
○ How would business be hit if quicker payments were demanded?
○ Is a regular check maintained on purchase ledger balances / extent of credit taken?
○ Who checks goods received against invoice? Is method used both cost effective and secure?

## 11. Costing (see Chapter 5)
○ What method(s) used?
○ Who is responsible for supervision and amendment?
○ What items are costed? What items are estimated?
○ Do they use their own historic costs / their own estimated future costs / costs provided by an outside source?
○ Are forecast costs regularly re-examined?

○  How accurately are overheads assessed? Is method of overhead recovery logical? Is it suitable for all products?

○  Is an allowance made for scrap, wastage etc?

○  Is *full* cost of labour allowed for?

○  Are actual results measured against standards set? How do target margins compare with actual results?

○  If estimates are given do these allow for subsequent increases in raw materials etc?

○  Is marginal costing ever considered? Are contributions of individual products known?

○  Is allowance included for use of assets not shown in balance sheet e.g. machinery fully depreciated?

○  Is too much time spent controlling insignificant costs?

## 12.  Pricing (see Chapter 6)

○  Who is responsible?

○  What are pricing strategies?

○  How are prices determined?

○  How frequently are prices reviewed and amended?

○  What are major bars to more frequent adjustments?

○  Is market research used?

○  How price sensitive is market by product range?

○  Comparison with competitors?

## 13.  Working capital management (see Chapter 12)

### a.  Stock control (see also Purchasing above)

○  Who is responsible?

○  What are stock holding policies for: raw materials / components / work-in-progress / finished goods?

○  Safety levels / lead times / reorder points / reorder quantities?

○  Obsolescence?

○  Storage facilities?

○  Security: what are weakest aspects? Is stock readily saleable?

○  Control system good? How often physical check made: are variances common / uncommon?

○  Stock turn: improving / declining?

○  Is control cost effective? Is more regard paid to high value / high turnover items? Is ABC system appropriate? Does 80 per cent / 20 per cent rule apply?

○  How is stock valued?

○  Are changing levels of consumption monitored?

○ Are stock-outs frequently seen?
○ Are stock tax relief provisions allowed for?
○ Is insurance adequate?

### b. Debtor control

○ Who is responsible?
○ What is overall objective? What are target credit allowed ratios?
○ What are normal terms of trade?
○ Are credit limits set?
○ Are status enquiries made? And rechecked periodically?
○ What is bad debt record? Is this bad? Or too good?
○ When is invoice sent?
○ When is statement sent?
○ What is collection procedure?
○ What happens to disputed bills?
○ Why/when are credit notes issued?
○ Are discounts given – why?
○ Is ageing analysis completed? Record of debts more than three / six months old?
○ Can progress payments be requested?
○ Are deliveries stopped at a particular point?

### c. Creditor control (see also Purchasing above)

○ What is policy?
○ Is suppliers' financial position considered?
○ Are discounts taken?
○ Is check maintained on totals outstanding to major creditors?
○ Joint ventures considered?

## 14. Information systems

### a. Management reports (see Chapter 14)

○ What information is necessary to run business effectively?
○ Is it prepared? In reasonable time?
○ Do reports include: outstanding order book / sales analysis / direct costs / stock changes / overheads / profit?
○ Who is responsible? Are they trained?
○ How do internal accounts compare with audited figures?
○ Is distribution list appropriate?

### b. Profit budgets (see Chapter 8)

○ Are these produced?
○ Who is responsible?

○ Who sets objectives and key tasks?
○ Are objectives appropriate?
○ When are budgets prepared?
○ How frequently are figures up-dated?
○ Are variances monitored? By whom? What action is taken?
○ Are budgets used as targets? If yes, how far down business is this so?
○ Are assumptions recorded? Is inflation allowed for?
○ How realistic is budget? How does it compare with past performance?
○ Is business being stretched? Is maximum contribution being obtained from scarce resources?
○ Key is sales forecast – is this realistic bearing in mind all circumstances?

### c. Cash forecasts (see Chapter 10)
○ Are these produced?
○ Who is responsible?
○ Are figures based on profit budgets? If not, how have assumptions been made?
○ Are all *cash* items included?
○ Are all assumptions reasonable, e.g. is forecast debtor payment pattern similar to what has happened in past?
○ Are bank charges included?
○ Is starting bank balance reconciled?
○ Are variances monitored? By whom? What action is taken?
○ Is stock holding policy likely to vary?
○ Are forecasts used for planning capital expenditure and investing short-term surplus?
○ Do the figures add up?

## 15. Bookkeeping systems
○ What books are kept?
○ Who is responsible?
○ Is detail adequate?
○ Are books posted daily?
○ How often are trial balances extracted?
○ Has system kept pace with growth of business? Proprietary systems considered? Computer linked systems considered?

# Index

# Notes

# Notes

# Notes